INTRODUCTION

I can't think of anything worse than to be called a 'Saint,' or to go through life without breaking the law or testing the boundaries. My affair with the ballerina was only the tip of my doings. Fire-bomb my palace and send electric chickens into my church, but celebrate your liberty in this creation, for glory's sake. Fling your camels of rock beyond the doors of the ages. *These are my final words, so mark them well!*

Landru September 2017

DANCE OF THE RED-CROWNED PRINCE

From another place they flew,

Like dinner guests,

Dressed in black and ivory.

Beneath the ice-capped caldera,

Starved with cold,

Their piercing voices aimed at Outer Space.

Shrill-throated to the gowning sky,

And grouped in quaking melody,

They jinked and whistled,

For the lagging Star.

For one whose *will* bestrode the drouthy night,

Appeared upon the lake in chords of blue,

And who with sceptre and with light,

blessed his royal head with roads of flame.

CONTENTS

P1 Introduction P 3 Home page: *Official Web-site*

P4 You-tube videos P5 Home Secretary P6-8 Bog-paper

P9/105/107 Belinda's Hot Air and First Contact request

P39 Read all about *IT!* P49 A voice from the past

P58 HILT P59 Fanny by gas-light P60 Fifty years from now

P61/63/66/69/92/96 Ram-art P62 Scrooge P64 Normal Lamb (too timid and scared to run for Party leader)

P67/102/106 ZOO P88/94 Lost Pages P91 Interference

P94 Little Lord Fauntleroy at home in his palace

P97 Pensions   P98 Surgery P99 In Cathedral jars

P100 SEXPERTS P101 Will P104 Arc

P105 Roy/What's the point in daydreams?

P106 How to run your neighbours down/Yvonne up-date

P109 <u>Biography</u>

Copyright AG Enterprises 2017

Third EDITION (With added bile)

Home

Welcome to one of the most unusual and intriguing sites on the net.

The Literature section comprises several different HIVES each containing a selection of short stories, poems, and political satire.

There is also a section involving Prophecy and Prediction, Spells and Invocations.

You can even order your own personalised ASBO.

I have long considered writing to be a form of art. The Artwork section contains pages from the infamous 'THUNDERBUCK RAM.'

BELINDA'S HOT AIR gives participants of the site the opportunity to express their views on a very diverse range of subjects. By clicking on the heading you can add your own comments, but you will need to be signed in to Facebook.

FIRST CONTACT is a forum for new untested art forms and experimental writing.

In an age of increasing state control and monitoring your general comments and feedback are positively encouraged by the genuine and the brave.

Our freedom of speech and liberal values should be permanently fought for or else they are lost.

Live dangerously and to your heart be true.

Proxima Centauri Alpha L0+4A

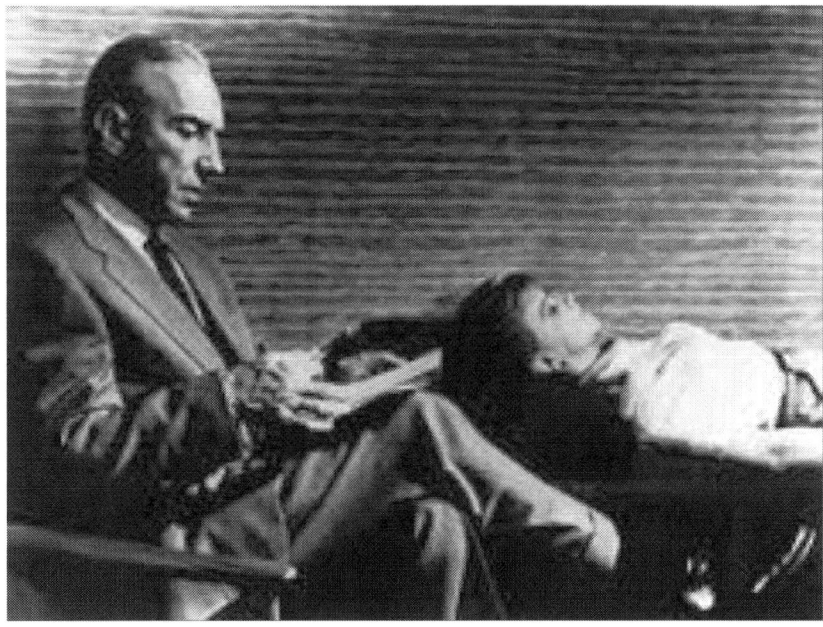

On You-tube tonight:

POLICE HARASSMENT SUPPORTED BY GOVERNMENT
Police Harassment: **BALDRIDGE'S BARK WORSE THAN HIS MOUSTACHE**
POLICE SOCIAL WORKER in tangle with dangerous crook
BALDRIGE FORGETS WIG BUT NOT SLEEPING CURFEW
POLICE HARASSMENT (BALDRIDGE RETURNS)
POLICE HARASSMENT Grumbleby and Co (Final bit)
POLICE HARASSMENT Waffen SS Grumbleby (5)
POLICE HARASSMENT BY DORK AND CADFISH (3)
ARIAN GRUMBLEBY POLICE HARASSMENT (4)
ARIAN BUMBLECHOOK AND GOOK CONTINUED POLICE HARASSMENT (2)
BALDRIDGE BACK to harass, cajole and subdue (Supported by Government)
POLICE HARASSMENT OF PENSIONER WITH ALZHEIMER'S
POLICE HARASSMENT of alleged Sex-Offender
How to deal with persistent ass-wipes
POLICE GANG CALL IN FOR FURTHER TRAINING ON PORN WEBSITES
POLICE HARASSMENT BY ARRAN GRUMBLEBY NORFOLK PPU
Mafia hoods widen search for camiknickers
PINKY AND PERKY LEARN HOW TO DANCE (or to belly-dance)
Harassment by Police Tossers in the home
SAD
Beekeeper signs register accompanied by choir of angels
Beekeeper pursued by swarm of giant bees
Born again Christian cult
Two bee or not to bee

I wonder how long it will be until you give them yet more powers to pry, spy and cover in poo?

BUNDERCHOOK STARWORD POET
THE HOME SECRETARY
Military Historian Simpson
Police Support and Empathy Unit,
House of Commons,
LONDON.

Nine years ago I contacted an ex-partner who I didn't even want when we slept in the same bed. It was not malicious or threatening. There was in fact one land-line call and one disputed text message. The police applied for a SOPO order linking it to an exposure thirty years before and convinced the Magistrates I was going to commit a serious sexual offence against a member of the public. After returning from prison for the phone contact I found that the police had been round the whole neighbourhood and every single person I had known to say I was a dangerous Sex Offender. They have continued to do this for the last nine years. Seven years ago they tried to put me in prison for five years for using a library computer after someone used a social networking site when I had forgotten to log-off. Following this I was given permission to use a computer at the library for *research*. The Plebs also took me to Court for not letting them know about an on-line alias and for not informing them about an e-mail address I had set up two years before. I was fined about £500 and ordered to pay a *victim compensation charge* because I was a Sex Offender.

A month ago they told me that if I used a library computer again I would be in breach of my SOPO because they no longer had the staff to monitor everything I did at my local library and I could be imprisoned for five years.

After ousting me from where I lived with the help of the Housing Association they continued to harass me at my mother's address and regularly raided our house at all hours of the day and night to make a detailed search of my bedroom. My mum was extremely ill at the time. I wrote to the nearby *Royal hand shaker* Keith Simpson, but he just shrugged his shoulders and implied that if I couldn't afford a Solicitor it was tough. When I tried to join the 'University of the third age' they informed the organisers that I was a dangerous Sex Offender who could not be allowed near women, even though I have been in a close loving relationship with my partner for over six years.

They continue to hound me wherever I go:

- Interfere with my post
- Pry into my e-mails
- Monitor all my on-line activity
- Attempt to block my writing
- Stop me from expressing my opinion
- *Have failed to question the Officers who beat me up at the side of the road over the phone contact and who made regular visits to my ex-partner while I was incarcerated
- **Plead with the Government for yet more prisons, tougher sentences, and still more Officers to chat, prod and grope...**

*Written on behalf of Mr. Cyril Blunderbuss: Outcast, criminal, nad, and public nuisance.
Signed: *Arthur C. Clark: bombast, McColl's Newsagents, Floss and Offal, No Cocks Yard, DEVON.*

BUNDERCHOOK STARWORD POET Amazon UK

BOG-PAPER

(One of nine calendars found in mum's bedroom).

Grossly patronizing Art-teacher

> 20 June 2017
>
> his is Genevieve I have got mums internet on, the wi
> ere in wrong and restarted her g mail as she could
> emember the password. So you should be able to t
> o her on Skype again.
>
> hings have been difficulkt for mum this year and she
> as had some problems with Andrew and there are a
> f concerns, both from me and from the community
> ut there are a lot of people watching out for her and
> ooking after her,
> peak soon Genevieve
>
> 29 June 2017
>
> Hi Jenny and Kevin. – and Chris and Doreen yesterday.
> Been ill again with an anti-fungal infection which was
> awful but the doc has delalt with it well and the terrible
> temperature and red skin has subsided but I am still o
> medication.
>
> Gen has gone back home Sunday. I went to the usual
> bible study group with my friend.

You recently advised me to allow mum to have all her own way if it makes her *happy*. You also implied it would help to keep the peace. Why in that case did you hit the roof when she went in your room last time you were here to push us all around and proceeded to cook you clothes in a broth of caustic soda?

We had a visit from *good son* Kevin on Bank holiday Monday. He isn't a blood relation, just a hanger-on. I'd just returned from my art exhibition at the Hall. I asked him why he always took mum's side, even when she was hurrying manically up the loft ladder looking for the cat. I told him that one of his aunties said no-one would be daft enough to believe a word she said. He replied: "It's best to err on the side of caution…" I think he's just trying to keep in with her. I'm unsure what he was implying. I tried to talk to him again today but he said he had "heard it all before…"

Give me your arse. I'm taking you to Emmerdale...

Hello,

Our Customer Service department here at the elusive ARENAL UK headquarters didn't receive the e-mail message below. If you still need help, please visit one of the pages below so we can quickly provide you with additional information or give assistance via e-mail or phone. Your Account provides quick access to open and completed orders and other account information.

'WILL YOU PLEASE STOP SENDING ME INFORMATION ABOUT ARENAL PRIME AND TRYING TO TAKE MONEY FROM MY ACCOUNT. I HAVE TOLD YOU SEVERAL TIMES I DO NOT WANT ANYTHING TO DO WITH IT. I AM PASSING THE RESPONSIBILITY FOR THIS ONTO *YOUR* LINE MANAGER.' *Mr. Angry*

PROHIBITION OF GAMBLING

The Big Brother Commission on anti-social behaviour have fined a gambling company six million pounds for not preventing their customers from spending wildly on their gambling site. Gambling as we know is an extremely wasteful and unproductive activity. It will also give you a bad name and you may even lose your seat on the church council. Life is not simply about taking risks or acting foolishly in pursuit of wealth. The trinkets of this life are worthless unless you already have them. Ask any mealy-mouthed Nanny of the State.

Bure Valley zoo barbecue

By Godfrey Winklebacker | Published: August 26, 2017 | Edit

I was sat opposite Janine in the lounge when we came in from the rain. Janine is a former marathon runner and was once pursued by David Beckham (Or so she says). She is a few years younger than me, but already uses a Zimmer-frame. Her huge upper torso towers over her frame as she shuffles omnivorously around the bins and garden. Today she was wearing a denim frock with buttons down the front which must have started its life as a cleaning tool. I know she has degrees left right and center, but it was the hungry looking orifice staring from between her hirsute thighs which troubled me the most.

SWAPPER

By Godfrey Winklebacker | Published: August 26, 2017 | Edit

I've told you about him before. He once went to school with a glass marble and came back with a train-set. His exploits as a gangster in my home town are legendary. He told me he was once beaten up by a gang of skin-heads when he went in the Palace coffee bar with his friend. 'Swapper' waited until he could get each one of the gang on their own to extract his revenge. I've seen him beat a bloke half to death just for owing him a half-penny.

Synchronicity/GIRL POWER

By Rumpelstiltskin | Published: August 25, 2017 | Edit

Once again, the two main soaps on ITV have similar stories and characters:

1 A husband who raped his wife on their wedding night and who is visited the week after his trial by her in prison:
"Pierce has no power left. He's just a pathetic man. Insecure, with a nasty temper!"
2 A man who is told on the eve of his mother's wedding that his father raped her and that he is the result. A fine young man, tall and handsome.

"How terrible for you mother! I hope I am nothing like him inside." Duhhhh!

DAVID

By Rumpelstiltskin | Published: August 25, 2017 | Edit

Think I'll stop watching Corrie because of that little cunt.

The Gas man

By Rumpelstiltskin | Published: August 25, 2017 | Edit

The Gas man came today. He said: "It all looks fine Mrs Amis!"

"In that case you can fit me a brand-new boiler costing thousands of pounds," she gleamed.

Comments

SAINT JUSTINIAN THE GREAT
(Holy Roman Emperor 527-565)

By Usuli Twelves | Published: August 18, 2017 | Edit

Byzantine Emperor, who sought to revive the greatness of Rome and to unite the different parts of the empire. Was helped in his quest by Empress Theodora a former lap-dancer, who by all accounts was very good looking and excellent in bed.

Because of his conniving ways, during some horse-racing in his honour, the crowd rioted, and surrounded him in his palace. He was about to escape by boat, when his wife persuaded him to stay and call in his special troops. As a result, thirty thousand citizens were massacred on the ground, encouraging him to lead the *Italian campaign* and reclaim land from the savage uncivilized Visigoths.

A truly memorable person, with Christian leanings, and proof if any were needed that the wonderful human species has not changed in any way since its inception.

*Early Christian kings soon saw the utility in becoming Christian. It gave them greater authority and control. It led to a consolidation of their power. It proved there was a god who looked after their interests.

"Allahu akbar!"
By Sarin | Published: August 24, 2017 | Edit
Go on then! Shoot me. You lily-livered Mayor of the rotting foundation stone.

Thank God for Doctor Gillam

By Sarin | Published: August 23, 2017 | Edit

Doctor Gillam has a grey beard. He is tall and slim, is calming and relaxed. He's a good doctor. He doesn't try to rush you or make unpleasant innuendo. He didn't appear to have any 'issues.' He heard all my complaints and helped me with every one, listening carefully and professionally, accepting me as I was. He didn't even mention his salary once. I felt a lot better for seeing him.

No such thing as 'hate' crime!

By Sarin | Published: August 23, 2017 | Edit
What the ass-holes in Authority call 'hate' crime is really nothing of the sort. First of all, hate is a very emotive word. What people usually mean is dislike, or dissimilarity. An objection based on a different point of view or outlook. I can't stand Leeds United fans because of their dense nature, but I don't actually *hate* any of them. Most of them were born like it.
We all live in a very competitive world. Are the Authorities really saying that hate is wrong, that we shouldn't disparage our enemies, that we are not allowed to put them down? That's about as stupid as saying there should never be any more war or conflict and that peace/ineptitude is the final solution for everything. Yet more invasive laws to control the populace.
Why can't I bloody well hate someone if I want to??

One way to do it

By Sarin | Published: August 23, 2017 | Edit

I noticed the pine disinfectant standing alongside mum's mouthwash in her bathroom. They are both coloured green. If you were tired or in a hurry you could easily get them mixed up.

Doctors and nurses

By Godfrey Winklebacker | Published: August 16, 2017 | Edit

Some Doctors have no time for you these days. Too busy bird watching to answer any serious questions or prancing around the room in their high heeled shoes and min-skirt.

Now that's a migrant boat I wouldn't mind coming ashore.

You can't con a Connie

By Rumpelstiltskin | Published: August 19, 2017 | Edit
Connie came round to pick some plums from the garden with her husband. If he's not a Christian martyr then I am Jack Lemon. Her face is almost as wrinkled as a Didwell. I said: "By the way, I'm Margaret's son…"
"I know who you are!" she scowled and went off in a huff.

Jews not greedy or arrogant
By Usuli Twelves | Published: August 17, 2017 | Edit
Why so many gold fillings then?

Ban all Arab drivers from owning a car

By Usuli Twelves | Published: August 18, 2017 | Edit

As we cast our eagle eye over the events in Barcelona, we at BUNDERCHOOK HQ overheard the following:

"You know this is wrong. You know it's not *right!*"
"We had to run for our lives. I never want to do that again."
"It's the most exciting thing which will ever happen to me."
"Everyone needs to *come* together!"
"We just want to have fun in the Sun."
"Evil men who will not escape 'justice.'"
"The sheer panic on everyone's faeces!"

Robert Mapplethorpe

By Usuli Twelves | Published: August 17, 2017 | Edit

Why should two animals drinking each other's semen be wrong?

Why can Michael Barrymore get millions for wrongful arrest while poor men get bugger all?

Famous footballer earning millions a week

By Usuli Twelves | Published: August 17, 2017 | Edit

Wouldn't be earning anything at all if the club hadn't paid off the girl!

Pikey Old Bill

By Usuli Twelves | Published: August 17, 2017 | Edit

I spoke to old Bill about his telescope, which he said was aimed at Jupiter and Saturn. I like the way he lifts his foot and holds it there for several seconds before putting it down on the sidewalk. He bears a striking resemblance to WC Fields but lacks a big cigar.

More mental health

By Usuli Twelves | Published: August 17, 2017 | Edit

More mental health nurses are needed:

1 To restore confidence
2 To control, manipulate and intimidate
3 To treat with contempt
4 To keep the keys

Trannies

By Usuli Twelves | Published: August 17, 2017 | Edit

I saw the man with the dog loitering outside Bure Valley Railway today. He was wearing high heels and a dress. Yesterday I saw him walking down Marriot's way with a handbag. I think it's terrible the way he's treated.

I always said that Stuart spent too long on his own.

Market Surgery Gestapo

By Usuli Twelves | Published: August 17, 2017 | Edit

My letter to the surgery asking to be involved in mum's care was completely ignored. No surprise really when you know how much gossip there is and with whom.

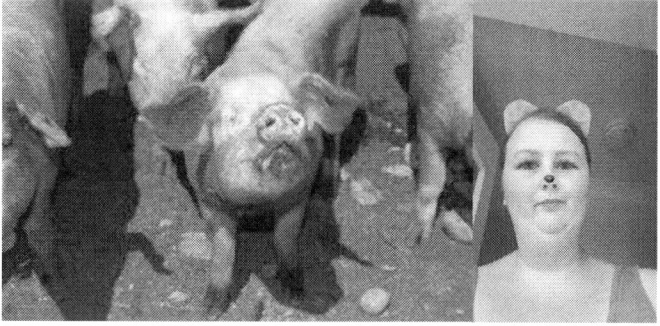

Gay men okay to foster children

By Usuli Twelves | Published: August 17, 2017 | Edit

If it was two heterosexual men fostering a little girl eyebrows would certainly be raised, but that is very unlikely to happen…deeply unfair and not worth the bog-roll its written on.

New developments on old manifestations

By Adumla | Published: August 17, 2017 | Edit

Mum is now doing her clothes in the sink along with the cups and plates. Her vests and underwear with their pads inside float around on the surface.

I know the church are very supportive!

Lord of the Rings

By Godfrey Winklebacker | Published: August 16, 2017 | Edit

George Michael
Boxing ring
Circus ring
Bull ring
Telephone

Chris Evans…

By Godfrey Winklebacker | Published: August 16, 2017 | Edit

I don't mind Chris Evans getting paid the most; he has a 'heart of gold.'

IF FARMS AND FARMERS GO DOWN SO DO ALL THE CITIES

By Godfrey Winklebacker | Published: August 16, 2017 | Edit

The red faced human egg known as 'Paddy' came pounding to the rescue and wrapped his arms warmly round her breasts.
"Pearce raped me! Pearce raped me!" she murmured.
Looks of horror. Sniggers from the gallery.
"You should never force someone to do something they don't want, even when you are married!"
Like shop round Asda's or listen to her droning on about her so-called friends…

Janet Head

By Godfrey Winklebacker | Published: August 16, 2017 | Edit

Totally blanked me when I said hello at the supermarket today:
1 Have I done something wrong?
2 What did I do and when did I do it?
3 Who's been sneaking to you?

Kim Jong-un gay porn icon

By Sarin | Published: August 30, 2017 | Edit

Some years ago, while working as a male escort I was invited along to meet a young man at a well-known ski resort near Geneva. We went up to his hotel room to un-pack his luggage, then I called for room-service. He was wearing an old Nazi uniform at the time and sported a quiff. He told me his name was 'Elvis.' I was surprised to find a small panda lying on his bed and an application form for 'lumberjack.' For the next few days I was paid to catch a number of adolescent choir boys. I also took him to see a couple of basketball games while I was there. He liked to wear his brother's old shoes and to smoke large Cuban cigars when no-one was looking. I caught him *moon-walking* into the lobby one day. A small brown monkey was waiting on a sofa. As he led the animal away I heard him say: "just wait until you see the length of my intercontinental missile!" And:
"When I am down on my hands and knees do you think we could do doggy-style?"
We exchanged contact details but I have not heard from him since I contracted aids.

Aylsham library manager

By Godfrey Winklebacker | Published: August 16, 2017 | Edit

Helen told me that they no longer allowed users to work 'off-line,' therefore I would not be able to use a library computer. "You will have to sort it out with the *pigs* for yourself!"
I suggested they have a 'MOST WANTED' board in the library entrance.
She stared through me as if I didn't exist.

Could you possibly lend me a pen?
And, do you have any spare labels?
Apart from the one I already have of course!

The poor man's Fred Astaire

By Rumpelstiltskin | Published: August 19, 2017 | Edit

Bruce Forsyth has finally left the stage after over seventy years of heroic: -

attention seeking

ambition

addiction to fame

tap dancing with his cap

Though he may have been a very mediocre talent more fitted to the music hall he did buy a tombstone for his great-great grandfather's grave. Friends in the business said that he was a 'national treasure,' and that he was adored by every young female who appeared on his shows.

Shortly before he died Bruce said: "without contact with my audience I have nothing…"

What a taxi driver sees in his mirror

By Godfrey Winklebacker | Published: August 16, 2017
I waited in line on a Saturday night, outside the Huddersfield night spot. They were stood in the rain. She ran into my black cab holding her hem. Her black leather dress gleamed in the streetlight while she fiddled inside her handbag. Along the dark lanes we sped, past the bird stained monument to Harold Wilson…I adjusted my mirror and waited for the games to begin.

Popularity contest

By Godfrey Winklebacker | Published: August 16, 2017 | Edit

The pigs have actually made some friends after accusing the council of 'corporate manslaughter.'

Joke shop
By Godfrey Winklebacker | Published: August 16, 2017 | Edit
We once put itching powder down a lad's back at school. It turned his back green and one day his cock fell off. Today I called in Mad Mike's biscuit shop. He had a few bikes knocking around so I bought one of them. I told him Chris told me it was cheaper at Dr. Feelgood's. *He* told me that Chris had been fired for soliciting during work time and that he had once repaired a bike for the Deacon. The following day he had fallen off and broke both his arms. He followed me into the road again. Yes, I think he probably is capable of murder.

Charity Worker

By Godfrey Winklebacker | Published: August 16, 2017 | Edit

Double Dee was in the paper for raising money for charity. She's the biggest back stabber at St Michael's church and she knows it!

Psychiatric wing

By Godfrey Winklebacker | Published: August 16, 2017 | Edit

Seems like a good way to get a roof over your head and a quick shag in the hospital grounds.

Floodlighting

By Godfrey Winklebacker | Published: August 16, 2017 | Edit

Thinking of getting some floodlighting so mum can continue her gardening during the night.

On-line grooming

By Godfrey Winklebacker | Published: August 16, 2017 | Edit

1 Anyone in?
2 You're cute!
3 Pull yer top up.
4 Slide 'em down.
5 Nice hedgehog.

Prince Charles only met Lady Diana thirteen times before they got married. That's a lot of grooming to get to your 'fairy-tale' coach.

The bliss of dispensing life sentences
By Herpes Zoster | Published: August 14, 2017

A few years ago, against weak to moderate opposition, the Government were able to bring in Indeterminate life sentences for dangerous villains deemed a serious menace to society. Forgive me for bringing this subject up again but nobody in power seems to give a toss.

1 Ignorant ass-hole Judges
2 Parsons on the parole board
3 Civil Servants so far up themselves
4 Screws screwing around and up to no good
5 Caged animals in captivity
6 Arrived in Court with a cocky attitude
7 Set a mattress on fire and slashed his wrist
8 Refused to do as he was told
9 Wouldn't take any more bull
10 Too smart to enter public school
11 Left to rot in a pool of his own urine
12 Not greedy or cunning enough to be a twat
13 Can't have a pen because he might poke himself in the eye
14 We found a photo under his bed Your Honour!

With prison numbers increasing by the bucket load and back-sliding Politicians tucking into their steak down at the club the customary status quo continues to fuel our scepticism. I watched his sister crying on the news. At least he had someone who cared, and she didn't think he was simply 'attention seeking,' after eleven years inside (*ten months for assault!*). The attitude of the general public has always been the same: if he hadn't done anything wrong he wouldn't be in there.

Care of the elderly

By Bird Dung | Published: August 12, 2017 | Edit
IT IS NOT 'ABUSE' TO TRY TO CHANGE SOMEONE'S CLOTHES WHEN THEY ARE DIRTY OR TO LEAVE THEM IN THEIR CHAIR WHEN THEY ARE SHOUTING AND SCREAMING. THIS IS NOT EVIDENCE OF A 'FAILING' SYSTEM BUT IT DOES SAY A LOT ABOUT THE PEOPLE WHO RUN THE COUNTRY.
*They even play with their own crap. sometimes!

What's the difference between an egg and a bloody good wank?

By Usuli Twelves | Published: August 13, 2017 | Edit

You can beat an egg!

Oh, Fk off Genevieve…

By Usuli Twelves | Published: August 13, 2017 | Edit

y parky gobbling git!

Better than expected

By Usuli Twelves | Published: August 13, 2017 | Edit

- As expected Brian rang his mum to say the police social workers had been round again and that they had ordered him to leave the shit-tip. It was about a month overdue. The sprog had been left with a neighbor while they rowed outside the kitchen door. Brian loaded up his weed and half a dozen cans into the back of the panda car. While his mum slept on the couch he vomited all round the bedroom. As a reward mum treated him to a slap-up meal. I was relegated to third place. The Sumo wrestler turned up the next day to beg him to come home.
- ***(Brian wasn't wearing his engagement ring because he isn't engaged. He said that Yvonne had "got engaged to herself!" In that case why write 'engaged' on your Facebook page?)***
- "Haven't you ever wanted any children?" he grinned. "Why don't you like them…" Brian *had* wanted to be a Copper when he was young.
- I told Chris I didn't want to talk about Brian all night or about his hemorrhoids.

*If I didn't want to talk about him then I didn't love her.

David Low to leave the building

By Usuli Twelves | Published: August 13, 2017 | Edit

Saw the creep sloping out of the supermarket with the 'Astronomer.' I would presume they were doing what they normally do on a Saturday, and that is spike all the baby food. If he's not a paedo I will eat my hat. He smiled at me as he loaded up his truck. Best news I've heard all year!

The rights of man *By Usuli Twelves | Published: August 13, 2017 | Edit* There aren't any.

Leo Zeilig

By Godfrey Winklebacker | Published: August 13, 2017 | Edit

I'm not sure who to tell about my relatives all ganging up to try and evict me. This is a repetition of events which have been occurring since I was but fourteen. The car is still being hidden at Jeremy's on Charles Ewing Close so we can't do any more car boot sales.
His aunt and uncle were always siding with the Establishment…!
~Always ask:
1 What exactly did I do?
2 When did I do it?

Bure Valley Zoo

By Godfrey Winklebacker | Published: August 13, 2017 | Edit

The Security guard in the office said I could go in the building as long as I didn't rape anyone and just so long as I was accompanied by my partner. I said there were no residents in there worthy of my attention and that I was free to visit whoever I liked. She didn't want to hear about our close escape on the road (Freak Temple had been in there to talk to her as soon as she heard I was back). I told her it was all about labels. Mine to be exact.

Terrorists responsible for Grenfell

By Godfrey Winklebacker | Published: August 13, 2017 | Edit

I would like to refute the suggestion that Muslim terrorists were responsible for the Grenfell tower disaster. We all must be aware by now that it was a faulty fridge which caused the fire and no incendiary device was ever used. I did not light a torch near the foot of the tower or blow on the flames and neither did Mustapha Ali of Bridge Street, the Forge, Dagenham.

Statues in public places

By Godfrey Winklebacker | Published: August 13, 2017 | Edit

NO statues should be left to stand of anyone we don't like or who don't fit in with our perception of what is *'nice.'* Anyone unpopular should be torn down or have graffiti written all over them.

The Love Island girl

By Herpes Zoster | Published: August 12, 2017 | Edit

Burst into tears because *only* her boyfriend said she was the most beautiful.

David Davis worth his weight in gold
By Surloin Steak | Published: August 31, 2017
Britain is really up against it now, but we do at least have a shrewd and competent negotiator. The EU want to punish us all for leaving. How can someone be accused of not honouring an agreement, when they are no longer a member of the club? I have never once heard of anyone having to pay extortion money for departing a controlling and infuriating mob.
Who could not be irked at seeing Michel Barnier glaring stone-faced from his platform?
What does he mean by:
"It's not that I'm angry. I'm just determined!"
Determined to ruin our economy for shrinking the power of Brussels!
I mop my brow and thank the lucky stars that we made the right decision to vacate this doomed and bureaucratic organization in the first place. Please don't give in to their threats!

Chilcot in love with Blair
By Herpes Zoster | Published: August 12, 2017 | Edit

Chilcot says that Tony Blair was 'under strain' when he went to war in Iraq. Nice to know the boys are all looking after each other once more. How come the poncy old Judges never allow any of us to use it as an excuse to kill, maim and piss-take?

MERKEL 'very angry' with Trump
By Bird Dung | Published: August 12, 2017 | Edit

1 Didn't let millions of Muslims into the country
2 Said the UN was frigging useless
3 Refused to be intimidated
4 Thought others should share the burden

Why do Facebook never answer?
By Bird Dung | Published: June 19, 2017 | Edit
Ever tried writing to Face-book. Have you ever received a coherent response?
WE KNOW YOU ARE THERE
WE KNOW WHAT YOU ARE DOING...

Ramadan van-man
By Bird Dung | Published: June 19, 2017 | Edit
extremist and extremely dangerous
a sickening and 'evil' human being, worse than an animal
should be driven out of society...

Keeping the pressure on

By Bird Dung | Published: June 19, 2017

The idea is to keep the pressure on, until they finally snap, when you can shout: "we told you so!" Then you drag them down the dungeons and beat the crap out of 'em.

Celebrity strip

By Surloin Steak | Published: June 14, 2017 | Edit

I wonder just how many famous celebs will be brave enough to doff all their kit off before an admiring audience of millions in tomorrow's live television programme? It wasn't that long ago that the pigs would have be racing round to arrest them all for 'indecency.' How times change...

Andy's review of 'Fearless'

By Surloin Steak | Published: June 14, 2017 | Edit

'Fearless' is a new television drama about a man who has served fourteen years in prison for a crime he didn't commit. His whole family are against him, his son doesn't want to know him, and the girl's parents are refusing to let her body be exhumed so they can find the real killer. Complicit with all this trash are the State dossers. Tossing away behind their CCTV monitoring equipment they are doing everything they can to prevent the truth from coming out and their part in this miscarriage of so-called 'justice' becoming common knowledge. Someone asked me today what this story was all about. None of it seemed to make any sense. It's about "lying bullies and *shameless pieces of shite*!" I said. "Time you woke up isn't it?"

Getting old and dangerous

By Sarin | Published: June 14, 2017 | Edit

Getting old is no fun and is ruining my health. I drop into the supermarket and forget the cat-food yet again. I keep forgetting to turn off the cooker. The smell of burning's in my hair and mouth.

Bure Valley Zoo

By Bird Dung | Published: June 11, 2017 | Edit

I returned to the Bure Valley Zoo on Saturday to attend a garden party in honour of my memory. Pam and Heather both said they had missed me. Harry the 'Gnome' said I "never changed!" and half the other people there wouldn't even look at me INCLUDING Fat-ass, who had a black eye. The Bearded lady was sitting in the lounge next to *Graham ten-bellies* while I had a game of darts. She said to me: "it was a set up from the start. I know that now!"

Stupid beer swilling fanny-heads

By Rumpelstiltskin | Published: June 10, 2017 | Edit

If young people think we should stay in the European Union, then why did they vote Labour? The Labour policy is to leave Europe as well: there can be little or no difference between them and the Tories on how that would be accomplished. Certain Members of the Labour party also favour a quick departure. Student debt only has to be paid back by those earning a large salary: the reward of having a degree. We are now facing a European shambles!

Blast them right off the planet

By Peter Smith | Published: September 3, 2017 | Edit

If I advise President Trump to blast the Korean leader straight into orbit, along with his many toys, sycophants and gadgets would that be breaking the law? In a free democracy it shouldn't be a problem. But when did that ever exist?

Please, please, wipe the smile off their face!

Tall man fired over Mexican wall

By Sarin | Published: June 8, 2017 | Edit

President Trump doesn't suffer fools, even those in large brogues and sombreros.

Labelled at the library

By Godfrey Winklebacker | Published: June 5, 2017 | Edit

I overheard a Chinese lady joining the library at Aylsham. The 'Sue' told her that she could not bring anyone into the library with her who was of a certain age. I asked the lady what the Library Assistant had meant, as there are always new rules being added to monitor and intimidate us.

The 'Sue' immediately whipped her head round:

"If you have anything to ask about library rules you must ask a member of staff!" she glared.

"Not with your attitude," I replied, and walked straight out of the door.

About ten minutes later I was out in the garden trimming the bushes.

A Pleb helicopter raced across the sky towards me and kept circling overhead.

My fingers were soon employed in the usual manner.

CORBYN THE 'RABBLE-ROUSER'

By Surloin Steak | Published: June 10, 2017 | Edit

How can anyone call themselves a *radical* or anti-Establishment when they want to throw yet more money at a crumbling National Health Service, let alone employ thousands of extra Plebs in the *service* of the Community?' What are beer-swilling sociology students doing voting for a tribe like that?

Latest review of Coronation Street

By Surloin Steak | Published: June 6, 2017 | Edit

My name's Bethany and *I like it a lot*:

Last night we were meant to feel sorry for poor Bethany, who had been 'groomed' regularly since she first set eyes on Nathan. Nathan is a really wicked crook, who seems to take pleasure in seeing her shagged by a few local Coppers. Not once did I hear her cry out; "take that tiny prick away from my gob!"

Audrey Horsehead, and Lolita Mum both have her best interests at heart. If she goes on having sex with different men she will have totally ruined her life! Her boyfriend is very controlling, which means he would make a great Politician or Town Planner in the future. The conventional opinion is that she has fallen in love with the wrong guy. If only she had found someone like David Dwarf, or Thick-head Gary. She could have done so much better for herself!

I'm sure the Cops will come up with something to stick on him!

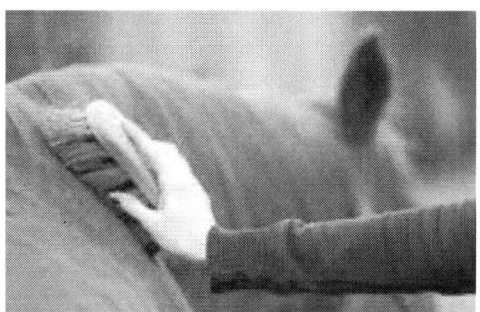

Confessions of a High Court Judge

By Herpes Zoster | *Published: June 6, 2017* | Edit

I met Judge McKinley in a public toilet eight months ago. His wife had just died and he was thinking about ending his life. 'Joseph,' as he likes to be called has been in the profession since his early twenties. I think he was just looking for a bit of company; someone to talk to. I told him that anything he said to me would remain 'strictly confidential.' We met for a drink at his club, and then we went for a game of snooker. I liked his honesty, and the way he was able to chat openly to me about some of the ass-holes in his circle. Joe would *lie quietly on the bench*, while I jotted down a few notes, or anything which came into my head. I'm looking forward to relaying some of his views back to you soon.

More Stalinist Flat-foots to keep us safe
By Bird Dung | Published: June 6, 2017 | Edit

We are told that it needs twenty pigs to monitor one individual, all on salaries which would make even a Doctor blush. With the current population that would mean about two million snooping, prying bullies to look over the shoulder of every Muslim family or cutlery merchant in the country.

What's the *good* in racism?

By Herpes Zoster | *Published: June 6, 2017* | Edit

When I was a youngster my uncle befriended a boy in the next street. There weren't many Packers living in town at that time, so there was quite a bit of name-calling and prejudice. It was a working-class town with lots of slums in the Centre. My uncle started helping 'Abdul' to do his math's homework. He didn't know how to do fractions.

When my Grandfather heard what he was doing he marched out of his house with a red and furious look on his face. I told him the number. It was near the house where a hundred men slept all in one room and a middle-aged white lady called 'Dot' worked as a housekeeper. I watched my Grandfather get hold of my uncle by the scruff of his neck (my uncle is a Chartered Accountant in Canada now) and drag him all the way back home. It's the only time I ever heard him swear.

"We didn't fight in the last war so they could take over the country!"

What's the use in 'racism?' It keeps the bobbies happy.

As I sit here burning…

By Peter Smith | Published: May 25, 2017 | Edit

As summer approaches, I begin to feel a certain amount of remorse for some of the silly childish things I did in the past. For instance; I was once on holiday in Torquay, many years ago: it had been scorching every day, with the weather actually getting hotter as the week progressed. The three of us were sunbathing on a little patch of grass right on the sea front. The sun was beating down. The breeze almost zilch. Our friend 'Bigsy' was sunbathing beside us both and had fallen fast asleep. He was a scrawny, occasionally irritating bean-pole of a lad with wavy ginger hair and a deliberately awkward disposition. He had a disgusting habit of gobbing on car windscreens. His main preoccupation in those days was with his baby's arm which he just couldn't seem to stop showing off. As we glanced at his back and shoulders a proliferation of huge green splotches were starting to appear on his scarlet body. I wanted to urgently ring a doctor, but we spotted a couple of chicks on the other side of the road so we ran over there instead. When we returned about four hours later with a few cans of beer we sat on a bench close by and waited for him to wake. No-one should be woken roughly from their beauty sleep! By then the splodges had a kind of radio-active glow. The sensible thing would have been to beat them all off with a brush. When Bigsy eventually revived he screamed and writhed around on the grass until we could find a nice hot bucket of saltwater to take away his moans…

*In the interests of honesty, I should just like to point out that while we were waiting for him to come round we were in fact discussing the whereabouts of his brother Gerard's big toe. We couldn't decide whether it resided at the back of the lawn mower, or whether it had taken root in the soil…

Due to the way memory is maintained it can be manipulated and changed over time. Surely, this has huge implications for us all. Our brains can invent memories which never took place and experts in the field can distort our thinking by planting bogus information.

'Into the flames with the wise-woman Mr. Parsons. We'll have a confession, or I'm not a Catholic. The whole village needs to be purged of this sanctimonious bullshit, or I'll have you both racked and pilloried in front of King James.' ➡

Hundreds of so-called 'witches' were hung or burnt to death during the reign of King James 1st of England who blamed the wreck of his ship on the evil spells being conjured against him. Most of the accused were simply people who refused to believe in the nonsense he did, such as the new edition of his bible. Hound-dogs of the State are still around today: hunting for delinquents, being paid to track down anyone not attending mass on Sunday. One of the main pre-occupations of the Witch-finders was to discover the witch's mark (not to be confused with the witch's 'teat'), which resided somewhere on the body of the accused. It's funny how often the mark could only be found at the top of a thigh or on the arse of the poor woman. Sometimes it even nestled among her pubic hair. Workers employed by the King knew for sure that the mark was caused by the devil's claw raking across the witch's flesh or by her being licked omnivorously by the horned one in places no-one should ever visit on Good Friday. Rooted in the politics of the time no doubt, but a worthy lesson in dogma and hysteria for those living on planet earth today.

Trump out for the count

By Herpes Zoster | Published: June 1, 2017 | Edit

I was just wondering if anyone had any better ideas to discredit the Trump administration than the horrendous suggestion that Trump had shared a glass of vodka with the Russian President and had read a copy of Anna Karenina?

The Good old days

By Usuli Twelves | Published: June 4, 2017 | Edit

I remember my Aunty Betty getting lippy with my Grandad in the nineteen-fifties. She had been out until ten o'clock at night and was just sixteen years of age. They began arguing near the bottom of the stairs. He took hold of her, led her into the kitchen and put her over his knee. Then he pulled down her knickers and gave her a thorough spanking with his bare hand. I bet he could have spun her around if he had wanted. She never answered him back again!

Right said Fred

By Bird Dung | Published: May 30, 2017 | Edit

Fred Bates came to work for my step-father in 1987. He was aged about thirty-four, with large sideboards and a handsome appearance. I found him charming and extremely honest. I found him very easy to talk to. He was always very hard working but something of a Lothario. He laid the flags on the new building site above Shipley Glen. He liked a cigarette and a pint of *Timmy Taylors*.

In 1991 he married Gillian, who was a friend of my step-father's. I never fancied her much myself. She looked too much like my own mother.

Gillian already had a daughter from a previous relationship. A small diminutive little waif called Tracey who came down with her mum at home time to collect Fred's lunchbox. Her daughter was aged about eleven at the time I first met her. Before too long Gillian gave birth to another daughter: Diane. And then a year or two later Winifred was born.

Fred continued to work for my father on and off. I heard that he often worked away from home. Then I heard that Gillian's eldest daughter, Tracey, had broken her arm in a fight in the kitchen. Tracey beat her mother up on several occasions and seemed to take pleasure in putting her into hospital.

When I heard that Fred had been accused of having a relationship with Tracey I could hardly believe it. It wasn't so much her age but her appearance. I was unable to understand why a man of his caliber would be interested in a girl like that. According to Fred, Tracey had seduced him at the age of fifteen while her mum was outside putting out the washing.

Fred was sent to prison for a few years for having sex with his step-daughter. In the meantime, his eldest daughter was being screwed by a man her mother had met in Pakistan.

While he was in prison Fred hung himself. He thought he had bowel cancer, but it proved to be false.

What a wonderful species we are!

London bias

By Sarin | Published: June 2, 2017 | Edit

'If the London herd don't like what they hear then their policy is to overturn the majority.'

Murder of the 'innocent'

By Adumla | Published: June 2, 2017 | Edit

The young and vulnerable are attacked because the strong are too powerful.

Comments

Life's what you make it!

By Adumla | Published: June 2, 2017 | Edit

If you fail to get rich and powerful it's all your own fault
If you work hard all your life you will be rewarded
Ask too many questions and you are really in for it…

Chesney 'Sourchin' the Corrie loser

By Surloin Steak | Published: June 1, 2017 | Edit

With a sour faced smirk young Chesney stared into the face of his former girlfriend. If only they could lead a 'normal' life.
"No-one would hit their own father. There must be something wrong with him!"
Which goes to show; he *is* just as dense as he looks.

Johnny Rotten

By Rumpelstiltskin | Published: June 13, 2017 | Edit

I was at a gig in Leeds in 1985 when I lost my guitar. When I returned to the hall I saw Bob Dylan taking something out of a box.

"What's that little cunt doing up there?" I said.

Communicating with ducks

By Peter Smith | Published: May 31, 2017 | Edit

It's important to know that communication on the net, or on any remote device, can cause confusion and upset if not properly understood. A large percentage of communication involves body language, tone of voice, etc. It's very easy to misunderstand someone or misinterpret a joke for instance, when no offence was intended.

I like grooming ponies

New law

By Adumla | Published: May 30, 2017 | Edit

You aren't allowed to hurt anyone's feelings!

Break in the ozone layer?

By Adumla | Published: May 30, 2017 | Edit

That explains why my face turned bright orange, why it wept like a an amber rose and ran down the side of my ear, why my head grew to twice its normal size. Apparently, there was a break in the ozone layer last week which might explain why I ended up getting baked like a cake and why I swelled up like a blinking tomato.

A medium sized note

By Adumla | Published: May 30, 2017 | Edit

CLEAN THIS UP YOU MUCKY TWATS "SORRY"NEVER ARRESTED ANYONE CONSTABLE! LAZY GITS GREEDY GITS   NO MORE VICIOUS PLODS   GET LOST!   NOW DO YOU GET THE MESSAGE   PLANT FOOD

Shortest suicide note in history

By Adumla | Published: May 30, 2017 | Edit

....s

Tampering with private mail

By Adumla | Published: May 29, 2017 | Edit

Dear Mr Lamb (Liberal MP),
Would you be interested in answering the following query?
I recently sent a book of poetry and articles to a Member of the Liberal Party at the House of Commons. It did not have a bomb inside the package or any other device capable of causing harm.
The book was returned to me after being examined by an 'Off-site Contractor,' (Newspeak for collusion between the Post Office and the snooping Authorities?).
I have suspected this has been going on for some time. Do you have any opinions one way or another about the free movement of information?
Message sent 29 May 2017 **(no reply)**

Lost all my food

By Bird Dung | Published: May 26, 2017 | Edit

It was scorching hot here in Norfolk yesterday so mum turned off my fridge to see if all the food would go off. She is being nice to me all of a sudden. I have the sense of a knife being sharpened somewhere for greater penetration.

American cave bomb hits the mark

By Godfrey Winklebacker | *Published: May 24, 2017*

The biggest non-nuclear explosion of all time cleared out the rat infested cave system in Afghanistan and was hailed an outstanding success by the President even though only 90 Martyrs/Losers were vapourised. It is essential that all Insurgents be wiped clean of the map for fear they might contaminate all decent minded people across the planet.

In your garden

By Peter Smith | Published: May 23, 2017 | Edit

Reaching out for Vivienne

For about two years I watched you in the garden. Blue jeans, wavy golden hair. Small I thought. Quite petite. Your husband had a dark beard and looked like a big bad wrestler. Then you were all by yourself. From my window, behind my lace curtains I continued to watch. That's when I sent you the note. A mysterious note, from a stranger. Your next-door neighbour rang pretending to be you. After a short chat you came over for coffee but I blew it all when I tried to kiss you before you left. You wrote me a letter to say you didn't want anything more to do with me. I was working in a lonely Signal box. My own fault. I wouldn't have chosen a job like that if it hadn't seemed necessary. Most of my time was taken up lifting weights and trying to evade the Inspector. You rang me again a few weeks later to invite me round for a meal: "Just as friends!"

I helped you do some artwork for the kids at school and went round a couple of times a week. You were lovely. A friend of Suzanne Dando.

I don't know what went wrong after that.

I think the chap next door put me off.

A few months passed and then my name appeared in the paper.

I was cycling up to the gym when I saw you in the distance coming towards me. You smiled, a sort of awkward smile and you were shaking your head at me. Your eyes looked red and you looked as if you had been crying. That was thirty years ago, so why did you suddenly appear in my thoughts?

Confidential information

By Bird Dung | Published: September 8, 2017 | Edit

I called into my local Market Surgery. "Has my partner been in yet for her appointment?"

"Oh, we're not allowed to give out confidential information," smiled the desk clerk.

"In that case why are you always on the phone to the pigs?"

All Trumps fault now

By Peter Smith | Published: September 3, 2017 | Edit

- Acted defiantly in the face of tyranny!
- Rubbed a dictator up the wrong way
- Tried to prevent nuclear meltdown
- Threatened to take him down a peg or two

I see what they mean now. He is a force to be reckoned with.

Bure Valley animal sanctuary

By Godfrey Winklebacker | Published: September 8, 2017 | Edit

The mob were having their meeting in the lounge. Christine suddenly blubbed: "I just want to be loved!"

Horrendous attack at Manchester Arena

By Usuli Twelves | Published: May 23, 2017

- Scarred for life by the experience
  Shocked and saddened by the loss
  Shouldn't really have happened
  An 'amazing young man!'
  Very scary with lots of screaming and running about
  An appalling and inexplicable tragedy
  Fallen victim to an attack
  A pre-meditated function of the Caliphate
  A cold and calculated act
  Were all 'having a good time'
  Directed against the sweet and innocent
  An attack against 'innocence'
  Love is always stronger than hate!
  No responsibility of the Government
  Police van to get a new face lift
  Commissioner to get a new hat
  Abhorred by all decent law abiding citizens
  "Perfect in every way."
  Our thoughts and prayers go out to the families
  I was there on the day
  Andy Burnham out of his hole
  Smeared my eye make-up ruined my skirt
  Pouting at all the cameras
  Countless acts of 'kindness'

- ## SOP (Stinks of piss)

- By Godfrey Winklebacker | Published: September 2, 2017 | Edit

- We were sitting in the lounge at Bure Valley Zoo listening to Marian who had just rung the hospital about her stomach by-pass:
  "Is there anything you want me to do?"
  Talk quietly? The mob remained silent.
  I rose to leave. No-body was speaking to us any way.
  The stench of Graham ten-bellies in the corridor nearly made us vomit.
  I think he had just done a dump.

- NO COMMENT!

Wanted dead or alive

By Sarin | Published: May 20, 2017 | Edit

A pair of dangerous criminals were being hunted round the streets of West Yorkshire today. Beware! They will take the last bob you have out of your back pocket. The escapees are now believed to be on holiday in Florida and are wanted in connection with a string of thefts and muggings in the area.
* One of the suspects has recently been apprehended.

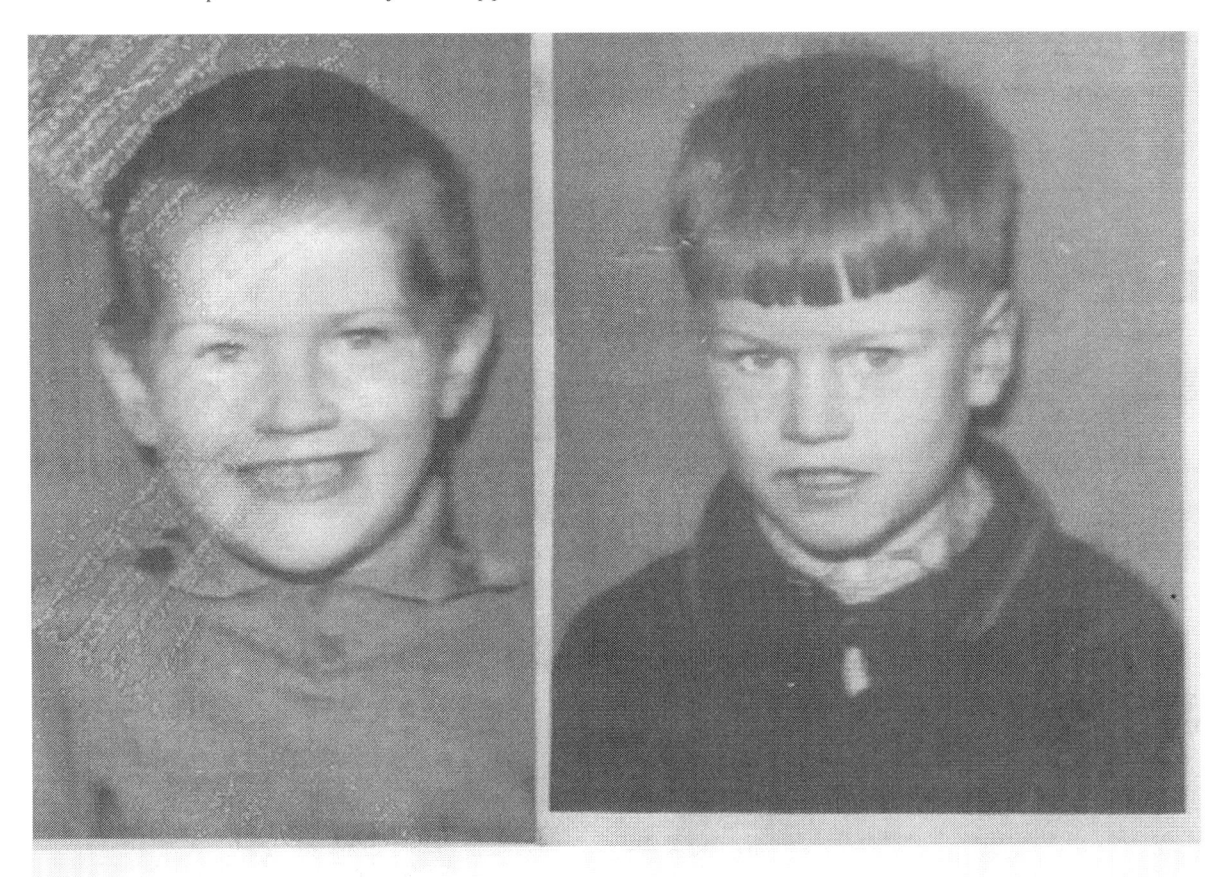

Where the Sun don't shine

By Bird Dung | Published: May 20, 2017 | Edit

You can take your boxes, your terms of approval, your fake smiles and your labels. You can take your recognition, your incontinence pads, and your tributes. You can take your Turner prize, your Green shield stamps and your remuneration. Your houses, your sports cars and your women. You can take your Sunday suits, your bow ties, your bowler hats, your dickie bows, and your crap, and stick it where the Sun don't ever shine. I really don't give a toss!

Beryl
By Sarin | Published: May 19, 2017 | Edit

When she came back from the wedding mum said:
"Beryl thinks you are a sweet little man and wondered if you would like to step out with her one day."
"What have you done with my keys you monster?"
Ah, I know what it is: she's feeling better and has been talking to the Vicar.

Grey seagull escapes ridiculous encounter

By Sarin | Published: May 19, 2017 | Edit

It's a long time since I've had the pleasure of reporting from Julian Assange's balcony. Good news this time. He will not be taken to trial, or even charged with rape, after all. His so-called victim says she was railroaded into going ahead with the case by the authorities. On this occasion, it didn't involve a bribe or the threat of a gang bang. If this had been Joe Bloggs from Manchester without any friends in high places you can bet your bottom dollar that he would not have been wining and dining for years at the Ambassador's expense. This whole story is beginning to smell like month old bog water. What kind of message is this sending out to the many people who have been taught from an early age that truth is important? Even the Met don't talk about 'fairness' these days. They are too busy speculating on the Stock Exchange.

Agent Peabody, who is well known to have the ear of the Chief Commissioner every third day, tells me that it is not uncommon for the Plebs to plant false evidence if it gets them a pat on the back from 'Mother,' or a rise in their conviction rates.
"Peabody! You will have to go," I holler through my loudspeaker. "They can plant the *DNA* where they like but they will still have flies on their shit!"

But *mark my words!* ~The odious slimy swarm, licking their chops on the street below, will find something to bring him down from his ivory tower. If it's not 'breaking his bail conditions,' for a crime he has not even been charged with, then it will have to be something else they have cooked up down at the pig-wagon. Be careful you do not drop a fag end or a Copper's ABC book from your balcony Mr. Assange…

Why didn't he want to go through a long and arduous trial to prove his innocence. Because he isn't thick? You mealy-mouthed servants of the bullshit.

Does anyone with an ounce of grey-matter in their skull take a blind bit of notice of any of this nonsense?

READ ALL ABOUT IT!

BURE VALLEY ZOO

The knives are out!

Catalogue items have vanished from the lounge again.

It must be Andy.

It can't be anybody else…

I've seen the 'Mehmet' crawling around outside so more lies must be on the way.

Chris said she didn't want to think about it.

I suggested Yvonne had a kid for us.

"Sorry?"

POXY OLD JUDGE SAYS 'SATIRE' KILLS

A middle-aged toff who offered a reward for someone to **do-in** a *Remainer* has been given a custodial sentence. His defence Solicitor said that it had only been 'satire…'

Free hi fi

Mum has given Keith's hi-fi away. It was valued at hundreds of pounds. I had it advertised in the EDP. She's up to her old tricks again, the little cunt.

Trump's son can talk to who he likes

I thought the **Democrats** were always looking for FILTH?

I wanted to get 'burnt'

I told mum that my head had got badly burnt in the sun due to a break in the ozone layer.

She said; "oh, you just wanted it to get burnt!"

PRIVATE MEMBERS BILL

Another excuse to suck up to authority and give yet more powers of arrest to the ignorant and pea-brained.

Deacon of Walsingham

While I worked in Walsingham years ago I prayed upon all the nuns I could...

Tell-tales always right

Mum had a phone call from David Martin the 'organist' this morning. That's the prick who looks like Rolf Harris. He said that it was an awful situation and that he was terribly sorry about what my mother had to put up with. The Church were all behind her! She told him that Social Services and a number of other agencies were involved, and that all sorts of people were concerned about her welfare.

The Dick said she could ring him any time.

I suppose that's what they call 'getting a fair trial.'

HERPES ZOSTER

1 Mum has taken away all my books and handed them over to the police. She has also destroyed anything else I have written that she could get her hands on.

2 Pain-in-the-butt has turned up out of the blue. I found her sitting in her nightgown. That explains why mum has hidden the car at Jeremy's.

3 Christine has a bad foot and cannot walk down any more.

4 Margaret Mildwater descended from the Act bus and scowled at my bike, parked against the wall.

5 I passed the Fat pot-bellied man on my bicycle. He called out; "I didn't think they'd have you back down here after all you did Popeye!"

Tried to run us both down on Station road the week before.

*Well, *they have let me back* you two-faced, red-cheeked chump of the cockroach!

6 Barbara Pardon had three children to three different men when she was married to her husband, and she thinks I have a problem.

7 South American schools have been invaded by a biblical plague of locusts resembling *Geoffrey Boycott.*

OPEN HEART SURGERY

George has just had open heart surgery. He's not the same man he was. I saw his car covered in bedding. He said he'd had a flood. That was in Bure Valley car park where he kept his dogs.

Paul O'Grady...is a useless piece of ...

We are told that Danny la Rue was *jealous* of his talent.
Pull the other one: it's got bells on!

GARDEN LABELS

Cocksucker   Your wife's a slut   About time   Mucky cunt   clean this mess up!   Fuck off Genevieve   You're a thick twat   Thick cunt   P Way tosser!   Soft as shite   demoted 2 dickhead   thank god it's finally over!

Sex fiend

Walked past mum and the bitch doing the gardening. They didn't speak and neither did I. If I spoke to either of them it would only give them an excuse.

Evil bomber

The Pigs are blaming You-tube for supplying the Manchester bomber with information to build his device. If only it was so easy!

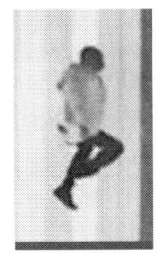

We love you Jonathan. Peace bro!

Bring back the birch

It's wrong to inflict pain on another human being, unless they are really nasty of course!

Highlight of the day

Seeing Andy Crick on Norwich road out cycling and slapping the back of my neck. He shouted: "you're a cheeky twat!" And you're a born again Christian!
I don't suppose that will be the last we will see of him.

Attitude of the ambulance men

After four hours of headaches and feeling sick I rang 999. Two men marched into the bedroom. One of them said that I was 'under investigation.' He roared at me when I couldn't keep my eye open with the torch shining in it. The grey bearded one snapped:

"What do you mean you don't know if you've had a *stroke* or a heart attack?"

I rang my mum to tell her the ambulance was there but she put the phone down.

I suspect she is colluding with the pigs again.

A thick Wellington

Dr Wellington spoke to me at the surgery today: "we are compelled to inform the police about anyone feeling like taking their own life. I am not here to discuss politics."

"How about I make a referral to the psychiatric department if you are *genuinely* feeling down?"

Don't bother. I've had enough of your frigging labels…

Patient's Support Group (Market Surgery)

WE WERE NOT ABLE TO PROCESS YOUR APPLICATION.

Influence of the Sky

Politicians complain that the electorate are being influenced by on-line material.

So they can be the only ones to make you do as you are told.

Twats in the family/blood pressure through the roof

My 82-yr. old mother was talking to my relatives in Canada on Skype. She told them I had stolen all her jewellery. She said I was terrible to live with and that she had told the police I wasn't wanted there. My aunt and uncle told her to get rid of me as soon as she could.

I told them they were both "thick!" and it didn't matter if they were University Professors or not. (*In a previous incarnation I was 'Assistant rat-catcher'*).

School seclusion

A boy was placed into seclusion for having a skinhead haircut. Wanker teachers!

Visit to St Michael's

Mum: "I know you're here!"
Vicar: "You are welcome to stay, but it is traditional to take off your hat."
Me: "How do you know I'm not a bishop?"
Mum: "Where's my wheelbarrow?"
Me: "In the garage where you left it!"

Quote from Leo: 'Jesus was a working class Jewish homosexual.'

"Do this in memory of me!"

Red squirrels

Killed off by the greys. Is that the same as the blacks killing off the ....?

TOADCRAFT

A few Christmas's ago I dropped in for a free meal at St Andrew's church among the tramps and down-and-outs. I was tucking into my meal when I spotted a former work colleague staring white faced in the distance.

MODEL ALLEGES RAPE AND KIDNAP

Great way to raise your profile and establish your body as a viable commercial product.

FAT POT-BELLIED MAN

Keeps calling me "Popeye!"

A worthy partner for the crazy obtuse *Whispering Woman*.

FIRST NIGHT WITH LIZ

"What's wrong with you. Are you gay?"
"Aren't you gonna shag me?"
"Why do you come here if it isn't for sex?"
"Please don't leave me here all alone."
(Prior to me being sent to prison twice for 'stalking')

BONEY M

TERRORISM OFFENCES

Freedom to speak your mind and get arrested

Okay to be left but not to be right

May cause upset and de-stabilization

Only if we give you permission

Not if you're a member of our Armed forces

Could be gay but not deliberately a cunt

TWO LEGS GOOD FOUR LEGS BAD

OLDER MEN

The girls at school said they preferred older men because they were more mature and able to drive. And that's not the only thing!

Thirteen-year-old taxi driver father's nine

MODERN USE OF SLAVERY

- Kept in poverty
- Liked living in caravans
- Not fit for human habitation
- Had to shit in the woods
- Holidays in Barbados
- Paid money for plastic surgery
- Worked hard for a living
- Came from a poor country
- Huge wads of cash
- Very dirty condition
- No relevant qualifications
- Poor career opportunities

NEEDS *'ANGER' MANAGEMENT*

DEFEAT OF ISIS

'Near the end of the century a leader will emerge who will unite the Arab nations of the Middle East. This will herald in a new age of culture, learning and prosperity.' **landru**

RADICALIZATION IN SCHOOLS

Children are about to be punished for thinking, for questioning and for answering back.

THERESA MAY

Ousted her rivals and then went crazy!

LIBRARY LEAFLET

'Nine years ago I was sent to prison for contacting my ex-partner on the phone. It was not malicious or threatening. I hadn't wanted her when we slept in the same bed yet the police applied for a SOPO order claiming I was going to rape someone. When I said this was nonsense I was ordered to 'shut up!'

Since then I have been constantly harassed by the pigs who threatened me with five years in prison for using a library computer. I had been going to the same library for years. They said they had insufficient staff to monitor me while I was there.

Library staff have colluded regularly with them and have continued to smirk whenever I go in.'

_T H E   J U D G E_

The Judge told me about a case in which a man was accused of raping his wife on top of a bus shelter during a Norwich City home game. I hear the man received nine years in custody even though his wife said they often went up there during half-time. While he was in prison the Judge's friends in the force paid the wife a visit as frequently as they could.

He's always moaning about how much money the drug's barons make.

You greedy old fucker!
I heard him in the cubicle again.
"I love you mummy."
"When is daddy coming?"

We cannot hear the other side of the story: that would be a continuation of the same offence according to the Oxford Times.

HOW DOES A STAIN GET TO BE ON A PIG'S GIRLFRIEND'S PAIR OF JEANS?

I don't know. How does a stain get to be on pig's girlfriend's pair of blue jeans…

I heard the bitch

Praises from my mum about my good behaviour have been short lived. I heard her on the phone again today telling Social Services that I was a delinquent who stole her bread knife and that she had been to the Cops several times already to snitch on me.

Back at the zoo (September 2017)

As an *incentive* for telling more lies about us kissing in the lounge and speeding on my bicycle Fatass and the Weasel have been rewarded by Wherry Housing. Their bungalow is the first to be completely re-fitted and painted in hogwash.

Guiseley Junction Signal box

Peter Farnell rang me on the internal phone shortly before he went down a hole in the road. He said that he was 'still able to do what us young lads could!'

CRICK-IN-THE-NECK

I saw Andy Crick emerging from the zoo the other day. As I was riding away I slapped the back of my neck. He chased me up the road shouting; "Just wait till I get you!"

RETURN TO THE ZOO

The Didwells went away this morning. I saw Tony packing their bags. We must have sneezed during lunch. Not long now until more complaints of sleep deprivation. I heard Marian say someone had 'de-sanitized' her bathroom... Harry the 'Gnome' was in the market place. Soon as he saw me he started whispering. His car drives itself down the High street.

Letter to Kevin (September 2017)

Dear Kevin,

Just to let you know: you will always be welcome in this house, despite you taking sides with mum and escorting her to the police station whenever she asked. I never felt any animosity towards you. I always felt we got along. What exactly do you think I have done to you? As I have said to Christine on many occasions, always ask:
1 What did I do?
2 When did I do it?

BOOK REVIEW 2 for Leo (An ounce of practise)

Shouldn't that be 'practice?'

Now I have read the book I should be able to do you a better review. The book was well written throughout. You obviously had someone to help you edit. I wondered why Viktor returned home to his partner when they obviously didn't get along. Was it just because of his daughter. Should couples stay together just for the children. A fresh start with a new partner might have been a better way to end the story. What did he actually achieve in Zimbabwe, besides the death of his friend and a good long hard shag with a *Tutsi* woman? You made the central characters believable, but I'm not sure if you would have been better introducing completely new names, rather than label them 'Nelson,' 'Biko,' or 'Hitler,' although the characters themselves were real enough. Surely this must be based on personal experience. You denied any of it was autobiographical... A modern book with modern themes, such as cyber-sex and the callousness of Authority. I think it would make a great film! I'm sorry your daughter has moved out to Australia. I noted too, how the main character suffered from hypochondriasis.

THINGS WILL GET BETTER!

NOW AND AGAIN

Now and again while sitting at my laptop I get a feeling of absolute 'dread' and nausea. It usually lasts about half a minute. I get the awful feeling the world is suddenly coming to an end.

Voice from the past

Hello Yvonne, just thought I'd say 'hi!' I am guessing that you are Walter's sister? I used to go to school with Walter many years ago and have never forgotten him.

06:44

Yvonne accepted your request.

Omg and I thought my brother was a saint. I am so pleased he lived a bit before meeting Anne. How old was he when he dated your sister? I had no idea he went out with Peter's sister. I never forget how Peter told me how he and Carlo had sobbed when they went to visit my brother's dead body. He remained a beautiful person to the end: a noble soul. I am sorry to hear about your headaches. Are you under a lot of stress? I am a very resilient person: something that I believe is bred into the genes of the children of immigrants but I am going to have to summon every last drop of strength to not fall into a depression over losing my job and having to start from scratch. I had quite a big job but worked for a dysfunctional man who basically bullied me. It was a psychological game of cat and mouse. Anyway, it is over and now I am keen to set up my own thing so I can control my own life and be there more often for my girls. Today the sun is shining over the lake. A perfect day for a swim. Switzerland is v beautiful. It would be great to meet and have coffee one day. Do you ever travel to London?

Drew   I think you have so much going for you Yvonne, that in the end the sun will shine through. Look at the magnificent things you have achieved already. You have a lot to be thankful for and even more to be proud of! Life has it's twists and turns. What may seem like a turn for the worse can eventually steer your life on a much more rewarding course than you would ever have realized. Walter was about sixteen or seventeen when he went out with my sister and Peter's. I don't think he got very far with Peter's sister and neither did I before him. That reluctance I had to get up on the stage at the St. Anne's Christmas party had three people in the story. Walter, who was trying to get me to go up and conquer my shyness, me, who despite all my bravado didn't like crowds, and Peter Mysko, who was wearing a cowboy suit very similar to mine, and who was beginning to laugh at my reserve. Peter went straight up without a single shred of self-consciousness or shyness in his body and pranced around the stage with my sister, while I watched horrified from the shadows. And I have never forgiven him for it! I have been under stress for most of my life. You are the only person I have told about that incident with the shirt. But I will never forget me and your brother racing around the streets of Blackpool trying to kiss any girl who came in sight. A door may have closed for you but a new door is about to open. Walter's birthday was just a few days before mine. I think it was about the 23/4 of January. To be continued...

Yvonne

Can I find your book on the internet? Would so love to read it.

Drew

That's alright Yvonne. I know what it's like to get a young family out to school on time. You would be shocked. Lol I am so sorry to hear about your dad! Wed 08:26

Drew

This must be destiny! I would so like to hear about your life, and how you managed to get away from Keighley. Did anyone ever tell you about the public speaking competition which someone put Walter in for? It came about by us all doing a classroom exercise. He turned out to be rather good at it. I was there when he first had a go. You had to write a speech on a subject of your own choice. He ended up going to some *grand finals* and was only just pipped into second place out of the whole of Yorkshire (by a girl I think!). It was the first time I think he had lost at anything.

Drew

**Another thing which springs to mind. (I hope you don't mind me getting this off my chest after so many years). I was walking along the side wall of St Anne's in the direction of the Town Hall Square, just after church, when Walter came walking towards us. I must say: he always looked absolutely perfect, and was always very clean and smart. My mother remarked: "Why can't you have *your* hair looking as nice as Walter's!" He took after your mum I think.
I told him what my mum had said, which may have been a mistake...**

'Hi Yvonne! Am having to hurry this because it's late. I don't have your time of birth for your *Ascendant*, but have come up with the following based on the information you gave me. According to my calculations you are an extremely sensitive person who cares deeply for others. You make a great mother and you are well loved by those around you. You are also very feminine. While in a relationship you put a lot of effort into making it run smoothly. You are usually a cheerful person, but you have your fair share of frustrations and set-backs. You have a cherishing and sympathetic nature and will guard your loved ones faithfully. You are tender hearted and generous in love. Good at looking after people. Your home is very important. I could see you being very interested in finding the 'right place to live.' You would be happiest working from home or being involved in a business which had your home as its base. Children and family bring you much happiness. If someone hurts you it is unlikely you will ever forget it. You do tend to dwell on things. On occasions, you can snap if you think someone is getting at you. You are proud of your home and although you like to travel are happiest within the safety of your own four walls. You reflect the people around you and are quite a thoughtful person. You would make a good orator or nurse, and a job caring for people in some capacity would suit your character traits. Funnily enough, you have Venus conjunct Mercury in Leo, which would lead you to be a smooth talker, and very good at any activity in which communication was involved, including writing. This would also help to make you a very creative person and encourage confidence.'

Drew

We used to play in a Subbuteo league together for a few years at my uncle's house and elsewhere. It was when your family lived just off Skipton Road, before you were around. On my way up to school in the morning, before we walked up Spring Gardens Lane together, to the Holy Family, I used to call at your family home, where I was introduced to herbal tea for the very first time. Your mum could possibly remember me. I was quite sweet in those days.

Yvonne

She certainly remembers you. She said you and Walter were very close.

Drew

I am back from the garden now. It's sunny but very windy. Am hoping to do another car boot sale in Cromer tomorrow, weather permitting and if mum doesn't hide the car. I am supporting her at the moment. My mum is in her 82nd year. I didn't sleep too well last night. Anyway, I have another snippet of history to tell you about. Me and Walter were quite competitive individuals. In the fourth year at St Bede's we had to take some exams to see what O-levels we would do. I was quite good at History, and did very well in the exam. We were given marks out of the whole year, which had about six classes, all containing about thirty odd boys. I was expecting a good mark and was pleased to get 90% joint tenth place in it. On most occasions 90% would be exceptional. Your brother Walter got 97% and 1st place in History out of the whole year (and we had some very bright lads in our year). It was all to no avail because he had to drop History to study Biology. You weren't allowed to do both.

Speak soon! x

Drew

Hi Yvonne. How are things? I hope you don't mind me giving you a few factual details. It's as much a test of memory as anything else. Have a nice day! Cheers, Andy xx

Yvonne

I absolutely love it. I am running a bit at the moment so will comment on what you wrote later. I have the feeling Walter put us in touch. I am going through a moment of profound change having just lost my job and I think there is some message here. Xx Thurs 16:37

Drew

I am deeply sensitive and intuitive. I thought I'd done something wrong when I didn't hear from you in so long. I wanted to tell you a story about when Walter just about saved my life. I'm quite an understanding person underneath. If you ever want to share anything with me I'm a good listener! Yes, another one! I wanted to give you something to remember about him by. Things that I remember which you didn't know.xx

Yvonne

Keep on sending me your memories. I often feel sadness for Walter. I feel like he had so much potential and could have achieved more had he not gone down the hard route of being a doctor. Also, Anne was an awful partner. He carried a lot. Do you know we are totally estranged from his son Philip. She turned him against us. You can google him. Xx

Drew

I try to write something every day, but not feeling too well. I used to do strongman tricks (but poorly these days). No-one could understand how I might be both a strongman and a writer. There was an air raid shelter in the yard. We used to climb on top of it. Walter was so fast he used to turn ahead of everyone and wave them on! It's one of the first things I remember about him.

I think we used to start back about 7th September. Have had a bad cold for a couple of days. I think I saw you in a dream a few days ago. I think it was you. Anyway. I have handed over three pieces of art for the exhibition today. I was running a writing group here in town till recently. There's lots of different types of writing you can do! **Thurs 12:19**

Yvonne

What was the dream about? And what sort of art do you do? You sound mega-creative! I did do an on-line writing course some time ago. I guess the idea should be to write something every day till you get into a routine. Blogging could be fun. How often do you write? My mum keeps telling me what a lovely boy you were. What happened? She says you suddenly disappeared. Was there some kind of disagreement?

Drew

I did know he had a son but I never met him. I have felt Walter with me sometimes, and not only in my dreams. I can be quite a spiritual person and probably have some healing gifts. I remembered the last time I think I saw you playing with your mum the other day. I was probably too shy to come and talk. We used to play football every weekend in the bottom field near the big Oak tree in Cliffe Castle. There was a sort of swing where you climbed up and held on, and then you ran along for a few yards. It was up by the top wall. I think I might have seen you there with your mum but I'm not sure when it was exactly. I always remember your mum. She was ever so nice! For Walter to be a Doctor would have pleased me enormously. I have known one or two personally, and they have always been among the cleverest and most intelligent people I have ever met. I always felt, like you, that Walter had the brains and the talent to be almost anything he wanted, but we have to accept the life we are given and he made his mark in this world for sure. A job like that carries a heavy responsibility. I remember seeing Anne a few times but I didn't know her well. Keighley was a rough town, and probably still is. I always thought Walter was too good for that town really. I may get in touch with his son some day. In the meantime I still have things I want to say to you. I just escorted my friend into hospital today. I cycled to Cromer and back. It was sunny to start with. I actually feel quite well today but last night was the return of the dreadful tired headache which makes me feel like I'm dying. I had two brain scans in the last couple of years but they haven't been able to find anything seriously wrong. What are your plans now you have lost your job? Do you think you will ever return to England. Do you miss it? You are lucky to live in Switzerland (I think that's where Lausanne is). I can see Walter's face as clearly as I can see my own and I have not seen him in over thirty years. I am just on the way down to watch Corrie at a friend's house. I look forward to hearing from you again soon, Yvonne. Xxx

Yvonne Just showed Mum your photos on Facebook. Of course she remembers you and sends you her love. X **Wed 23:07** Drew

That's nice. Thank you. X Ask your mum if she remembers Canon Holdright, Miss Garnet, Miss Tucker, Miss Lennon, Mr. Eardley, Mrs. Hodgekiss, Sister Marie, Sister Francis Savior, Monsignor Sweeney and any others....xxx **01:51**

Hi Yvonne. I might be off FB soon for quite a while so here are a few more reminiscences for you to mull over one day. I don't know if Walter is whispering in my lug-hole at night, but I've remembered all sorts of strange things. You mentioned Walter being a Saint. Well, he was, almost, but I do recall a little game we played in the break-times at St Anne's. I think it may have been myself who got him into such bad ways. We used to get in the front door and if no-one was looking go round kissing the statues along the sides of the church. I don't know why it should have caused us so much hysterical laughter, but it did. There were also our games of pontoon, Newmarket and 'brag' on the bus to St Bede's each morning which Peter Mysko always seemed to win; but then money was involved. I never saw so many fights break out over a game of cards. Peter Mysko could tell you more about it. Another memory which has stuck in my mind is my first drama class with Mr. Leadbetter at the Holy Family School. I remember me and Walter pairing up to do a short play. All I recall now is being extremely nervous in front of the whole class and throwing something (a shoe or a piece of paper) at Walter as part of the sketch. I think I was sitting in a chair playing an old man. At around this time he lent me his 'french/english dictionary,' which was just what I needed for my homework. It was a small blue book. He asked me for it back several times. When I did eventually remember to bring it in he said he didn't want it back and that I could keep it. I have had it with me ever since and it was in the drawer at the side of my computer until recently. When we first became friends at St Anne's there was an advert on television. I used to copy the advert in class with…."Aaaah!" And Walter would immediately answer: "Bisto!" I think it was for gravy. I booked us two tickets to go and see Led Zeppelin at St. George's Hall when we were at St. Bede's. It was a great concert. I think Walter really enjoyed it. I was trying to get him into rock music. My Uncle went along with us. I had made the mistake of getting my uncle a place miles away from us. We spent a lot of our time laughing at how static and miserable he looked below us. Walter came into school several times and told us how great the new television series called 'Monty Python's flying circus' was. I started watching it after that. It had a big influence on me. When I was about five years old I was standing in the underground at St. Anne's all alone and decided I better start talking to someone. I walked up to a boy who I had seen playing near me a few times and said "Hello!" The boy's name was 'Peter Mysko.' He asked me several times why I had done it. Well, there, after fifty-five years is your answer Peter. My friend Lydia said it inspired her seeing two such different characters sitting alongside each other at the dinner table. Peter had a very strong character and was a lot bigger than me. He was just a bit too boisterous for me to handle. When I was going through a very difficult patch in my late teens and was very unhappy he used to tease me a lot. We had a confrontation about an over-sized Levi jacket of mine which he wouldn't give back. I'm not the sort of person to hold a grudge, but that's why I have never contacted him. It was the only jacket I had apart from my school blazer.

- I TOOK WALTER TO PLAY BOWLS IN INGROW PARK WITH MY GRANDAD'S OLD BOWLS ONE DAY. HE WAS ALWAYS ASKING TO GO BACK EVEN THOUGH HE THOUGHT IT WAS AN ODD THING TO DO AT FIRST.

- Drew

Love and blessings to your mum! X

NB Your brother was renowned for his good looks. Some of the lads were sat around the far end of the school bus on our way to St Bede's. Mysko and the others asked him who he thought was good-looking. I was standing in the aisle way a few feet away because it was over-crowded. Walter said he thought that I was. I heard a few moans, and then Cahill and the others started laughing at me for blushing. Stick that in your pipe Genevieve!

Hello Drew. I am Walter's sister. I was very touched to receive your message. I still miss my brother. It was so tragic that he had to go so early in life but it is great that he lives on in our memories. Thanks for reaching out to me.
OMG! How lovely to hear from you Yvonne. I thought that maybe you never used Facebook any more. Did you see me standing next to Walter in one of my old photos. He will always live on in my heart. I hope to hear from you some day. Would it be alright for me to share some of my memories of him with you?

Yvonne: I would so love to hear your memories of Walter. You cannot imagine how much that would mean to me and no I did not see the picture.

20:31

Drew

I cannot believe how much you look like him. I suffer from migraine headaches Yvonne and aren't as fit and well as I used to be. Am at home all evening, but will have more time to reply later. I first saw you playing on a rug in front of the fire when I was approximately thirteen (actually I must have been about ten). Walter had invited me up to see you for the first time. I think you were a big surprise to everyone, including your mum and dad, who I remember very well. I haven't been to Keighley in years. It has mixed memories for me. I had a tough time in my last years at school. Am going to try and send you a copy of the photo I mentioned. All the best for now.x

Yvonne: Thank you Drew. Was Walter the boy on the left? Was this at primary school. I am sorry to hear about your headaches and some of your last years at school. Childhood is not always easy. X

23:33 A HIDDEN WOUND

That day in Blackpool was significant for me in quite a few ways. I remember getting lippy with some big guy on a merry-go-round and getting told off. Once again, I made Peter laugh. The three of us were often together in those days. There was another boy in our group called Stephen Hibbert. He had a bit of a nasty streak. I never knew how to take him. He was a bit of a bully underneath. I have always believed in standing up to them. Well, we had a photo taken in the pub. Peter or one of the others might still have it (I might have an old photo of us at Humphrey Head as well. This was an outdoor pursuit centre near Barrow-in-Furness where we went with the Holy Family. I remember me and Walter getting weighed and him criticizing me for not drying the dishes in the kitchen properly. I think he weighed even less than I did). The photo in Blackpool had me, Peter, Thomas Cahill, Walter, Hibbert, Kevin Thornton, and Gerard Wilkinson on it. I hated it. All you could see was a long piece of hair and a big ugly snout. On our way back to the coach I jumped playfully on Stephen Hibbert's back walking along the pavement. He threw me off over his shoulder, and as I was lying on the floor he ran up and kicked me full in the face. I fell into the road in front of an articulated lorry, but Walter ran forward and pulled me back just in time. I sat on the back seat of the coach next to Walter on our way home. He was very upset and concerned about me. He hated this Hibbert guy himself, and although it was not really in his nature, was forced to square up to him too sometimes. I had suffered quite a serious injury and couldn't speak for the rest of the journey, but refused to go to the hospital. For a long time my jaw clicked. I think Stephen Hibbert had in fact broken or fractured my jaw. Sorry for telling you! xx
I do get into London sometimes, but more of a home bird these days.xxx

Drew

Yes, that's him! I am still shocked to hear from you. There is a God! I was very close to your brother from the first time I went to school until about eighteen or nineteen, when he went off to college. I last saw him in a pub in Bradford when we were about twenty-five or six. He had lost some weight. We joked with him about it. I am a bit cautious about asking you what happened to him as I know it would hurt. A childhood friend told me she thought something had happened to him. I am sorry for being such a softy but I was upset for a long time. I have so many memories of him I don't know where to begin. Perhaps it was the time we had to go up on stage at the St Anne's Christmas party. I hid behind my mother and wouldn't go up. I don't think he would go up without me. Or the times we raced across the yard when we were so young. When I heard he might have died I tried to look his name up in the directory. Your dad answered, because I recognized his voice. I think he was still in the house on the far side where you had to go down some steps. I asked your dad if I could speak to Walter. All he kept saying is: "He's my son!" I am so sorry if I upset your dad. He was a good hard working man who made sure your brother completed his homework properly or he couldn't go out to play. When I was about thirteen your brother invited me up to tea. We had been playing football all day by ourselves in the yard at Hartington School, just a bit further down from your old house. We always did that for hours on a weekend. Your mum made me some pickled gherkin sandwiches for tea, which I thought unusual because I had never had them before. I hope you don't mind me sharing a few things which popped into my head. I don't have a bad memory for times that have past. It's the things which are happening now which make me all mixed up…NADSAT!

Hi Andrew. I am in Kos on vacation. The girls are with their dad in France. It has been a long leisurely summer. Time for me to think about next steps and how to rebuild things after losing my job. I am starting to feel confident that things will work out. How have you been? Have your headaches gone?
Not feeling too bad love. Just adding pieces to my Bunderchook page. I have missed you and wondered where you were. I hope your family and your mum are well.
What is your Bunderchook page? Your poetry? 22:27
It's a lot more than just poetry. lol. A mixture of political commentary, short stories and much more. I am putting some artwork into an exhibition at Blickling Hall this month. I have a link on my Facebook page which has some extracts: I was referring to that. I thought you had looked it up on Amazon UK. No matter. You are back. I did occasionally wonder if I had said too much. I am a great one for reminiscing you know. Some people may think it's a bit weird but I like reaching back into the past. I do have a life in the here and now, but I don't like to lose the past either, if that makes any sense? I have never been to Chios, but I have heard it's the nicest of the Greek islands. I do hope life works out for you. The changes you mentioned could lead you into a more satisfying and rewarding existence.

I have just started following your page so I can understand more of what you write about. Can you send me the poem you wrote about Walter. I would love to read it. I reminisce all the time about the past but sometimes it is so painful. What good came out of his untimely death? Nothing but sadness.

Feeling better today! Me and Walter were quite competitive individuals. We had a teacher called Mr Mulrennan at St Bede's. He was a sort of friendly giant, about 6ft 7ins tall. We had never seen anyone that tall before. He was a nice man though. Sorry if told you this already. We were in different classes for literature but both our books were always placed in a rack in the corridor, so you could go and see what the other one had got in his English essay, and the comments. I know for sure he used to see what I had got. I think I actually added comments to one of Walter's books once, as if the teacher had marked one of his essays. Don't worry: life will come full circle. As I said once before: you will end up finding another more rewarding path, but it may take a bit of time. You are probably being steered towards something much more satisfying and rewarding but it all has to happen when things are ready. You always have me to talk to. I am well acquainted with the madness factor in creativity. To be creative you have to stretch the boundaries. Tomorrow I hope to pop down

to Blickling Hall to see if they have hung my artwork properly. Just back from a barbecue. You could use the time you have to cogitate and take stock of everything. Sun 22:56
Are you ready to apply for anything yet or do you feel like a bit of a break? Do you have any ideas what you would like to do? I could do a bit of Astrology on you....
06:07

Astrology sounds great 👍
22:41

To do your horoscope I need your birthday and time of birth. I already know where you were born. It will give me some idea what the best occupations are for you. I hope you don't mind me reminiscing. I am cursed with a long memory! Have you ever read any Nietzsche? He teaches something called the 'Eternal Recurrence.' A bit deep for a Friday night perhaps. I do recall all the old lessons at St Anne's, but I learnt to question its dogma from an early age. I've done all sorts of things. I am even a trained Astrologer. I will try to find my old books. I could probably remember most of it from memory though. Don't be too alarmed by anything you read. I am quite out of my tree. It comes from having to challenge the human race over a long period. I refuse to let my memories die. My memories of Yorkshire are still alive! So is Walter somewhere. I still get my headaches sometimes and don't feel at all well some days. I am trying to get to bed earlier though. Walter speaks to us in our dreams now.

'We all have an allotted time in which to make our mark upon the world.'

How beautiful. I love it and the most amazing way to remember my big brother. Was there an air raid shelter? I always regard my brother as a post war product born of two refugees. When did you start writing? Do you write every day?

20 August 22:21

Drew
I'm glad you liked it. I wonder what your mum would think. **Mon 05:54**

Yvonne
I will let you know what mum thinks. I would love to write as well. Girls first day back at school so need to get started 😊

Tues 22:45
Thurs 22:22

Drew
I take a lot of interest in Current Affairs and like to write something on stories I hear in the news. Depends what comes up really. It's a mixed up troubled world for sure. Probably always has been. I think you should read as much as you can from across the world. I get the 'American review' delivered. I think it's good to keep a journal or diary wherever you go. Oh, the dream. lol. I am very interested in the workings of the mind. I saw you in a kitchen. There was a working surface in the middle. A door behind you which led down a path through the garden. I don't know where it was. You were talking to my mum I think. Don't take this too serious....it is probably my over active imagination, but you were blushing, or you were flushed. You turned and went down the path towards the gate. I think I tried to follow you, but it was as if I wasn't really there. I dream every day I go to sleep. I think good dreaming is essential for a healthy frame of mind. I think people like Peter Mysko used to laugh at me because I was always trying to look at things from a different perspective and I wasn't afraid to question the *status quo*.

Drew

I might send you a photo of my work at Blickling Hall! Hmm! lol. In the kitchen there was a sort of pipe or chimney in the middle. Okay. I admit it. I'm a *bit* crazy, but I don't care. Have a headache tonight Yvonne. long day! Keep well! x

Fri 06:14 Yvonne   Please do 😊 By the way: your dream could so easily have been true!

Sat 06:58 Yvonne

Madness is ok. Most creative people have to have an element of that. I am so up and down at the moment. Coming to terms with losing my job and now trying to find a new role is not easy. It is times like this I miss not having a brother or other sibling but like everything in life you just have to get on with it. I hope you are feeling a bit better. Try yoga. Do you think we will ever see him again? Xx

DREW

One of the saddest things I remember was being asked to do games when I was about nine or ten. I wouldn't take my shirt off. When I showed Walter the scars on my back he cried. I think he was confused. I don't think he could understand where they came from…

Walter always wanted to go out with a blonde. We picked up our first two girlfriends at a dance in Morton, but I got the blonde one. He wasn't happy with the other one. Everyone thought I was *cream-crackers* when I finished with her; because she lived in a mansion and I lived in a *scruffy old slum* with a nut-case for a mum. We had a party at my house when my mum was away at a teaching conference. I introduced him to a girl with curly ginger hair from Greenhead Grammar School. He disappeared so I went looking for him, only to find him in *my bed*...! "I do not believe it!" I was stunned. I can still remember his face as he turned round and the girl's dress half way up her thighs. He went out with this girl for a long time and she was very upset when he finished with her. I thought he could have done better. But it was his first real girlfriend, for sure. He went out with Peter Mysko's sister for a while after that. The man who I had been brought up to believe was my father had just tried to take his own life.

57

CHIP ON THE SHOULDER

While studying for my A-levels I suffered from socio-phobia and walked around school with my hand held up to my face because I didn't like the size of my snout.

I had just overheard my father say to my mother that he wasn't my father, and that he didn't want anything to do with me.

My English teacher, Mr. Delaney, said in front of the whole class that I could write as 'good as Shakespeare.'

My first job on leaving school was as a street-sweeper and dustbin man. I was leaving home one night to go for a drink with some friends when my sister's boyfriend attacked me for peeping at her through the bathroom door.

My mother told me that I had 'got what I deserved!'

Not long after I was arrested for fighting in the street.

Back to the zoo

Had a visit from Sue, the SHAP rep, today. When I went to remind her about the appointment at three o'clock she slammed her door in my face. She said she had never heard of the Didwells. "Oh, fuck!" she snapped. "I'm right in the middle of making dinner. I can give you both five minutes."
After reading my letter to the twats at Wherry she scolded me for mentioning the past and suggested I re-write it taking out all references to the previous fiasco.
"But this is all about the past!" I said. "Ask any of the Managers."
"Keep a low profile," she said. "Why don't you come to the next Resident's meeting? I'm sure no-one means you any harm."
And watch another brawl break out over who had taken the dinner money...You must be joking!

SOCIAL CARE COSTS

Should be paid by those who can afford them and not from General Taxation. Why should poor people pay for the rich and famous to pass on all their wealth to greedy siblings. Why do Labour chiefs who believe in sharing the countries resources oppose such a sensible solution?

Fanny by gaslight

My dad knew all about it.
EVIL KID BROTHER
I would like to make you all aware that I am not responsible for any of the following:

- ✓ Repeated and persistently offensive posts
- ✓ The theft of a wooden spoon from the drawer
- ✓ A tendency to exaggerate or tell porky pies
- ✓ Lapses of memory and forgetfulness
- ✓ The insertion of a firecracker in the Superintendent's ass-hole

✓
✓ **MAKES A CHANGE FROM HAVING THE TIP INSIDE THE HOUSE I SUPPOSE**
✓

Fifty years from now

Will you still remember us,
Fifty years from now,
On Marriot's Way,
On our journey from the town?

Hand in hand we walked,
beside the bramble bush,
With the skylarks singing overhead,
And scores of rabbits bobbing from their burrows.

The boy who passed us on his bike, late for school,
The group of tennis-players under the dark bridge,
And a family with their puppy dog,
Calling in the distance.

Will you still remember us,
Fifty years from now,
When we are no longer here,
To amble hand in hand...

With the honeysuckle,
And the ginger Tom,
And that disturbing Cop car
hovering in the distance.

bunker, with a conglomeration of rotting vegetables heaped on the armchair.

The chrome training bench had vanished without trace, and the iron barbells had disappeared or were beaten brutally out of shape. It would be a long while until he could continue with his French curls.

A mysterious note was scribbled on the writing pad addressed to the "nadir man." Since he had been sent to *Coventry* the clique constantly referred to him as the "Screwball." It simply meant a longer spell out of circulation. *Stylites Simon.*

Just as he was turning towards the booking office he suddenly noticed the "Area Inspector" spearing at warp speed up the statue of undergrowth on his blind side.

The hunter quickly entered the signalbox in three swift bounds instantly accusing P. of being indecently dressed.

The Inspector was wearing a consumptive grey suit which he fitted like a pipe cleaner's coathanger.

"Don't let me see you without your shirt again!" rebuked the 'Chinless Wonder' sternly.

"You must wear your issued uniform every time you are on duty."

"Balderdash!" snapped the Flash. "Are you jealous?" The man responded sharply. Had the grip of a Short Grandmaster.

"It's Mr. Stretch to you!" in a high pitched wail of an utterance...was he a eunuch?

"I've heard enough bad reports about *you* from your fellow mates. Not a day goes by when there is not another rumour. If your behaviour towards them does not improve I'll have no option but to drag you into the Area Manager's Office to give you a grilling on the rules!"

"Look at the disgusting state of this Shit-tip!" complained the Chinless Wonder, clucking his Adam's apple vigilantly.

"It never used to be like this until you got here." He suggested that P. had caused the *pretty kettle of fish* himself when he disclosed that Ynus had been there just before him.

54

SCROOGE

I had the privilege of meeting Scrooge at my job interview in 2003. He stood behind me the whole time while his wife fired questions about my work experience and character. His hair was like a frost covered treescape. For the last forty years he'd been Director of forestry at Oxford Brooke's University.

After that he took me on a tour of the new Asda superstore. The first thing I noticed was his swift and decisive manner. His face was like a Chinese road-map. I wondered if he'd had a lot of worries.

The previous Carer had been fired for arguing with him about some travel expenses and for reporting his son for down-loading kiddie-porn. *Scrooge* was what I would call 'the Prince Philip' half of the partnership.

We went to a gathering of the weird and wonderful over in Cheltenham. The hotel we stayed in had a superb, if slightly extortionate, restaurant. After gobbling down a great chicken curry he asked me if I'd had enough to eat.

Could I have another? He couldn't believe it when I managed to eat it all again, and neither could I. His wife looked uncomfortable to say the least.

Scrooge had a box of straws in the kitchen. After every meal he went round under the table sucking up any spare crumbs or bits of food. When the fruit went off in the garden he simply bit-off the rotting half and ate all the rest. I suspect he'd always had quite a prudent disposition.

His nephew told me about the time he had stayed at the house while they were away for the weekend. He had spent a short time speaking to his friend in Germany. About a month later the same friend rang him to say that *Scrooge* had rung them wanting to know who they were. I promised never to tell *Scrooge* what his nephew had told me, but one day I just couldn't resist the urge any longer.

One day his son made a mistake with my pay cheque. When I went to the bank I discovered he had written an extra '0.' I paid in my cheque wondering whether it was my time to quit the country. Shortly after this we returned to the house in Oxford. I parked the car as normal in the drive, then the phone rang. *Scrooge* asked me to check the car because he thought he had left his jacket behind. When I went out to look it was there on the seat, but underneath it was Scrooge's wallet, stuffed with fifty-pound notes. I counted them all: £200!

I went back to the phone to tell him I had found his coat, and that I had also found his wallet. He asked me to look after his wallet until he could call down. In the meantime I added an extra '£50' to the total.

With goose-pimples loaded on his white mystified body he swam once around the route just to keep his vellicating maulstick from suffering frost bite.

When the Flash at last made it to the event a large group of onlookers were gathered around the water's edge. The St. John's Ambulance were placing something on a stretcher from the deep chilling depths.

The white chloroformed body of a *jellyfish* was loaded on board as he called out despairingly from the van. Freedom of speech conformed to the norm. Had his head blown clean off. The 'man of steel.' Think devil. Flies on the same piece of shite.

"Where've you been all this time?" he pandered faintly. "Why does the fish plate take longer than my bicycle to arrive at any given destination?"

"Maybe it's time for a change," he tendered. "It's only because of you *infecting* me with your evil star that I'm in this rotten predicament. Well, say something, even if it's goodbye."

"I know," said P. "But never let it be said that I knew! One day all will be revealed. Loving their childlike follies their lies belie their frailty." [This new constellation; the 'Toad' named after him.]

"It's been scientifically proven! Only the good die young."

"Any mention of this and you'll be out on your ear!"

If he'd worn a suit of lead it would have been easier to see through his metal.

"You have a woman's cunning. If you'd been born with a *red nose* I'd have called you a prize bitch!"

Something totally uncivilized about civilized society. The persecution of rival factions.
"I don't want to know your reasons. Just shut the fuck up!"

Even the gods are cut down to size.
"I'd rather be an Arthur than a don Quixote!"

158

LAMB BLOG ON FACEBOOK

'I think Norman Lamb is the best British Politician in the country. He always speaks his mind, stands up for our National Health Service and serves the local community with all his heart.'

Like Comment

70

Norman Lamb and 69 others

Comments

Norman Lamb: Very generous. Thank you!

Like · Reply · 10 hr.

Heather Lee · Friends with Ted Gill and 1 other

Totally agree with you x

Like · Reply ·

1 · 10 hrs.

Simon Morley · Friends with Norman Lamb and 1 other

'If only my area had an MP like Norman Lamb. I was so proud of him today in North Walsham town center next to Frank Bruno. Why can't our other Politicians show the same sense of decency and empathy towards others?'

Russell Herring · Friends with Norman Lamb

You're hit the nail on the head! Gby

Write a reply...

Joachim Ryan · Friends with Norman Lamb

Agreed!

Marilyn Munro · Friends with Norman Lamb

Great guy. I voted for him but the other one got in. Now I'm voting Labour I'm afraid.

Henry Gee · Friends with Norman Lamb

'I am indeed afraid that you and *so many* other of my friends, who I thought were rational sensible human beings, are going to be voting for that Jew-hating, racist, terrorist-loving, traitorous cock-juggling spunk-trumpet Corbyn.'

Marilyn Munro · Friends with Norman Lamb/fed up of stacking shelves.
'I think you have been reading the Daily Mail.'

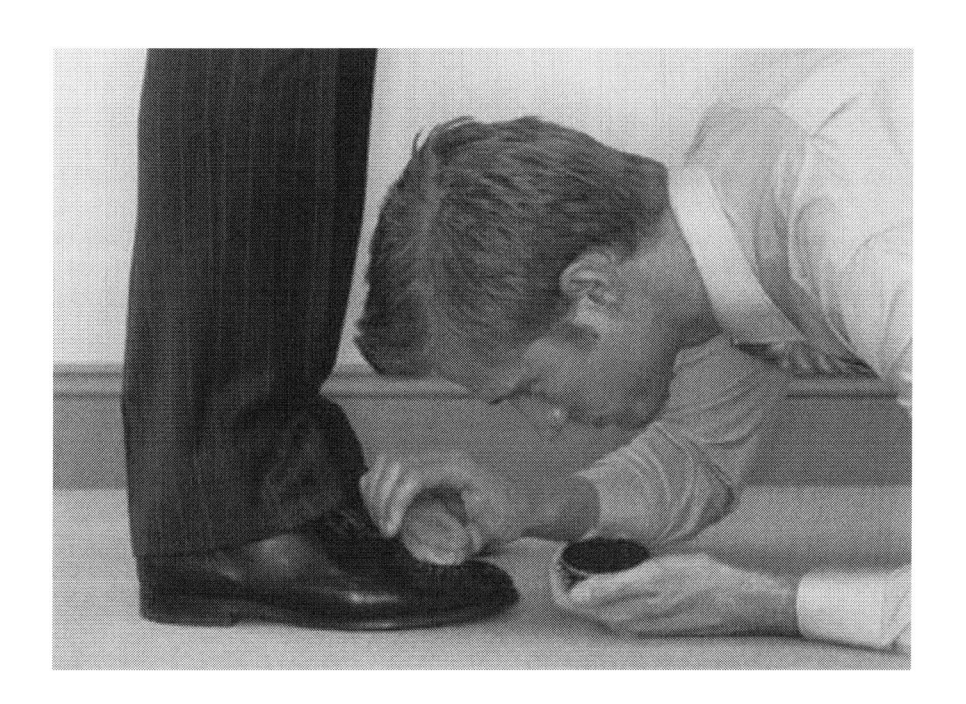

DEAR MR LAMB,

DAVID LAWS: I received a reply from the Security staff at the House of Commons. They had to send my book back without the MP seeing it because they said it represented a high 'security risk.' NO REPLY!

I hope you don't find it too distressing listening to anything other than flattery?

COMMENTS *If we had nuclear weapons you'd soon sit up and take notice.

Undiffled by the sour torments of the world I suckled you
at my heart. For I was greater than the follies of
your youth. Summer poured from my mouth.
    Sorrow poured from my hearth.
From the forest fringes I swept your tiny cove across
the bluebells furs to the shoreline.
    My beating heart beneath the giant softening spared
into the face of a glaring mammoth.
    Yes, I fled in the rain of an arrow. With a roar,
and a crescent, we were able to scale the heights.
    I will weather the storm, stem the tide and reap the
fruits over all the kingdoms of my earth.
    Where there is plenty I will bring want for all the
sons of unwanted child. For lover's Supreme !
    The chords of my hymn had been trampled into dust.
For I am the **sonnet of morphine
accidence**...

The Flashman suddenly hearkened, and found himself
still staring into the early morning dawn with the
church bells on the apex tintibullating vehemently. He
offered up the Yule-log. Antler scored palm. A cock
was crowing as Anus stomped across the threshold...
laid out on the deck were the ten obstreperous members
of the *lamping* gang who had evacuated the paddle.
    The refugees from the flood had gathered wearily for
shelter on the wooden tree stump of the landscape.
    "C'est la vie!" he shrugged. "But not as we know
it..."
    "If I ever catches who put those bloody *bluebottles*
in my ham sandwich I'm going to crucify him," barked
Anus.

F. felt for the clavis to the glass cage which was
normally hidden under the step, and opened the door, on
his second turn of duty.
    It had been cleaning day alright, but the Signal box
floor was covered in debris from the dustbin.
    His locker had been burst open and all the contents
had been systematically covered in black tar from the

53

Conversation heard at the Bure Valley Zoo (4/9/2017) 2pm

Present: Harry the Gnome, Marion Megaphone, Debra Dorcus and thin cockney, Keith Seems2good2btrue (soon left), Sleepy Sheila, (Andrew and Christine).

"When I went to sleep I went to sleep."

"I'm having trouble with belching."

"Enjoyed my fish and chips on Saturday but ate too much batter. Next time I will just eat chicken."

"I had a good dump in the bathroom but the toilet wouldn't flush."

"Janine gives me half of hers unless I want to be laid up for a week."

"Are you having dumplings with it?"

"I have a stew in my freezer to eat up."

"Wonder where Barry is today?"

"I prefer them done in the oven."

"I would really like to know how they make vegetable suet."

"Kate's expecting again. I didn't think she would be long."

"She's three so he must be five."

"They grow up so fast."

"George is like his dad. Charlotte is like her mum."

"It would be nice if she had twins. I don't think she'll mind what she has. Harry will be a Jack-the-lad. Why *can't* they try before they buy?"

"I don't like girls. They always get boys into trouble."

"Zara lost one. Harry's her cousin. I don't think Harry went there!"

"I'm glad I never had a girl."

"Here's my skinny friend from London who came last year. Neither of us are gay."

"It's always good to come together."

"My granddaughter's very ill…if it's a yeh they will try to put rods in her spine to straighten it up and with two heart conditions it's a very worrying time."

"A waste of money."

"She was told by the Consultant that titanium rods alone cost £18,000 each."

"Needs her heart working at the optimum level. Her kidneys and liver are all going to get squashed. She's only fifteen, it shouldn't take long to fall for one…"

"Before she's in the family way. She's 39% bent."

"They'll put the rods in and then she'll wear the plaster cast for months. It won't worry her much. She was out shagging again last night."

"She's the one who asked the question."

"She did it on the quiet so Ebony couldn't hear."

"Worth every penny these chairs. I don't think it's fair that visitors don't pay for them."

"Boys never grow up do they? They go backwards. Hahaha!"

"I'm thick. That's why I always talk in such a loud voice. It's funny to hear a Skoda hit a Lotus Elite."

"She said if you ring again I'll have you done for harassment!"

"Men are always picking their noses."

"They didn't find the onions last time."

"I had roast potatoes, chicken, carrots, onion, cabbage. The cabbage was lovely. Will should learn to eat less cabbage. Would cripple my backside."

"She didn't have a very good night last night. She gets cramp."

"I get it in my hand sometimes."

Burrhp!

"They didn't even offer us any cake!"

"They can stick their cake wherever they like ."

"Shut that door!"

"Another day gone…"

"And closer to Hell!"

"I couldn't move Harry."

"Good night Harry!"

"It's a good quality carpet. I don't think the next one will be as good."

(*Barry-the-Mute came in to see me but his Carer dragged him away*)

"YOU FORGOT TO TURN THE LIGHT OFF. WHAT'S THE LAST THING I TOLD YOU TO DO!?"

Oh, fuck off you big fat ignorant old cow!

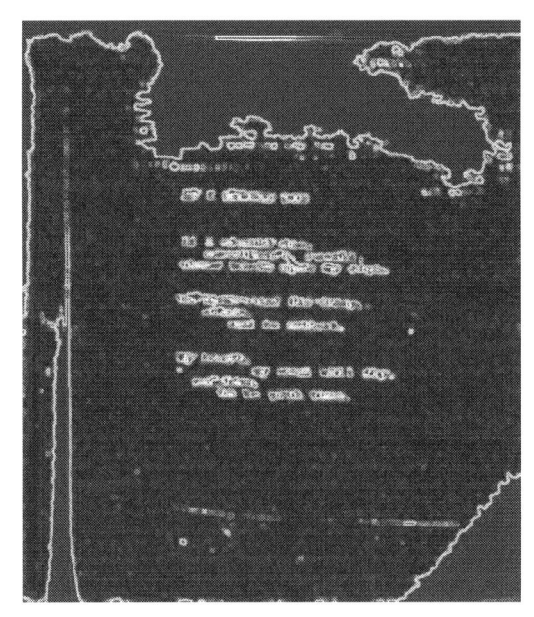

39, Bure Valley House,

AYLSHAM.

16th September 2017

Dear Wherry/Circle Housing (Specialists in Residential Care),

I am writing this letter on behalf of Christine Pigott, who finds it difficult to express herself in writing. She doesn't like to complain or cause a fuss, but since certain other Residents seem only too eager to get on the phone or make complaints I have suggested she start standing up for herself and let you know what it's really like from her perspective.

She told me that during the early hours of this morning (about 0130 am) she heard a lot of arguing and swearing going on next door. It went on for about half an hour while she was trying to get to sleep. Christine is not very well at the moment and this only adds to her worries.

This is not the first time that she has heard Mrs Didwell swearing at her husband or using the 'f' word. It's the type of language you often hear coming from next door.

There has also been a lot of banging coming from next door recently which has caused a considerable nuisance.

When I came in today (dismounting from my bike at the edge of the car-park) I could clearly hear shouting and arguing coming from the Didwell's kitchen.

Another concern which she would like to mention while we are writing is the situation which keeps happening in the laundry room. Christine keeps going back to get her washing only to find that the machine has been turned off again. This has been happening regularly for some time. The last time this happened (15th September 2017) she saw Vera Temple coming down the steps.

Vera said to her: "Have you got a problem?"

Christine had done nothing to provoke Vera, but then, as you know, you don't have to, because this is all about labels.

From experience Christine has learnt not to say anything to the people concerned because of the foul and abusive language which always ensues.

Yours Sincerely,

BLUNDERCHOOK

*NB I asked Chris what she thought. "Oh, I can't be worrying about that," she replied. "I have Brian's birthday to think about."

the head of livestock. Valt's tin motor was harnessed down to mud.

He banged his feet noisily against the nadir of the loft to give them time to climax before climbing to the top. He knocked on the windowpane marked 'Private' before pressing down the metal catch with a loud click.

A young man with a basin cut of raven hair was hastily adjusting his shirt while his auburn haired seamstress combed her hair in the mirror.

The brats remained completely motionless and continued to monitor the crescendo point on the screen.

Maxine rolled her dream clad eyes and touched her face still flushed from prolonged pairing.

Her drifting palps ploughed half cocked through the thrushes of her locks. She stared straight forward towards the door as F. immediately retired to the *Train Register Book* in order to sign on duty.

Valt grinned and replaced the knotted white handkerchief on his swollen summit. He informed F. that he was 'back with the missus' now that the charge nurse had given him the slip.'

Walter blushed and stared curiously down at the traces of *albumen* still sticking stubbornly to the arena of F.'s filthy fastener.

"I think you ought to know," he said. "The Signalmen in this area are gabbing about you all day long! It's embarrassing! I have to work with him I told them... One man's plight, is another man's delight!"

The *family of fugitives* gathered their belongings and piled into the hill-billy van while F. opened the brown paper parcel which had been flung from the Junction Library. Out of his tree! (o)...

The ex-booking lad had an unsettling habit of practically rubbing noses while he jaw-jawed, although useful tips of sound practical advice were gratefully accepted by the raw recruits.

An avowed athiest until his daughter's recent heroine overdose, which he blamed on the evil excesses of the inimical modern era, the *verandah tinkerer* had become a staunch advocate of the Rosicrucians.

46

Question 6 Does the *Virgin* drink huge quantities of beer to prove his manhood?
Question 7 Can the *Virgin* phleg further than anyone else?
Question 8 Is the *Virgin* a clever and sophisticated circumlocutor?
Question 9 Does the *Virgin* tell tall stories?
Question 10 *Prohibited!* and -p mowed of Pullant!!!

If you can answer the ten simple questions printed above and identify the insidious character in the photograph you could be on your way to winning a fabulous star prize!

All entries to be mailed direct to Mary Shithouse...

In the large bare waiting room a solitary heater pumped out its paltry energy as a dim lit *Will O' the Wisp* imposed a modicum of tinsel on the Alpine club.
Through the surrounding smog *frogs and fishes* rifled the railhead as she waited for the steamer to Larne.
Suddenly a tall sturdy gentleman broke in from the fell and shook his heavy mac against the radiator. He trailed his ancient vintage *tourer* across the room to stand against the plaster beside our hero's.
The distinguished midnight passenger sat opposite them and began pulling up his straps. He bent down to examine the competition with an expression of lionize.
The charismatic peer fingered the links of the superior metal article with his coy prestidigitator and verified they had been oiled sufficiently.
Like a sublime weighing scale he patrolled the pair of sleepy eyes with their mudguards incrustated from coom. Sometimes wished he could be 'gathered.'
"Going far?" he asked, picking sullenly at the grime. Come to the mad-hatter's tea-party!
He'd vanquished a few dragons in his time and had entered the *hall of the slain*.

"One day he discovered that he'd picked all't lining out of his cap."

"I knew his brother," nagged the "Riddler." "He caught the same habit and one day his head caved in!" They all laughed.

The clamour of their wagging tongues continued without desinence...but it was not long until they returned to their most favourite topic.

Anus suggested his gear might end its days on top of the village bonfire.

He gleefully recalled the time when the empty coaching stock units had been left to stand longer than was necessary in the sidings, as they attempted to keep him vapouring, while laughing up their sleeves.

The regular "Union Treasurer," pedalling his bachelor-of-science in systematic knowledge, always gave them a comprehensive report of the Flashman's ineptitude at the beginning of every shift.

He whispered like an old tart in a pub doorway about the day F. had missed his home station.

"And there he was!" chuckled the fellow with the face like the back of a tram smash. "I didn't hardly recognize him at first. As the train stood below me in the blasted platform."

"Flashing away he was, in broad daylight. I could hardly believe my eyes!"

Once more the heavy crew broke into unbridled mirth at the top of their vocal chords and a waspish silence rapidly ensued.

"Do you reckon he's flapping now?" hissed Furnace. "Let's give him a buzz to see if he's awake..."

Blip! Blip, B-l-e-e-p! went the whistle of the cable calling the code of the Bridge. F. flicked his button because he knew they would hear it click. For once they seemed to be talking sense.

Had he really heard all that? Should he confront them immediately and ask them what he meant? The stripling decided to appear in blissful ignorance and started on the line as if he had not been 'earwigging.'

58

He walked angularly to the portal where the moped rider would drape himself with the olive green mac and furnace goggles, throwing on his baldric and hob-nailed boots, before preparing to hike it up the steep meadow still in his PJ's...the scarf tied over his head gave one the impression of a Bunny.

In oblate seconds the twenty-two stone *Brobdingnagian* entered and angrily slammed the door in his wake.

It was a charm watching him attempt to dismount from his three-wheeler on the brow of the lane.

The walrus hair sprouting from his nostril could have easily been culled into a brush. Floss seemed to spring from his every orifice. Never had a day on the sick his mate said.

Anus had a bird's nest growing in his beard. He even appeared to be suffering from a deficiency of calcium. The relief was a natural supporter of the Gunners. He never swabbed his purple-and-white neck-rope.

"He's a dirty old twat!" he snapped.

The *Relief Box-man* raced straight over to the traces of ash on the floor where old Ernest had happily tapped his ancient tool, and blew his top. Flung open a case of his gaspers.

With his shirt tail still remonstrating over his enormous buttocks he lumbered over to the Block Bells.

He acknowledged the 3.1 for the passenger train on the solid brass tapper key before swinging the apparatus to 'Is Line Clear,' while studying the going form - flat to firm.

He passed the officer's special waiting in the station to the Junction, which was acknowledged by 3.55, for which he placed a 'reminder appliance' on the starter signal, before taking out his television set to watch the results.

Ignoring the trainee who might rob him of his *rest-day working*, the scruff, with bran still hanging to the underside of his belly, reported the time and unit number to 'Plank' on the traffic control switchboard.

42

Craftily burrowing deep into the mine-shaft he crudely unharnessed the holster of his ratchet slapped in the face by the source of all creation.

People said they were the 'windows of the soul.' As pretty as you like...Juliette's bonnie shades began to flutter like a pair of rabbit's wings.

He was evidentally out of breath. Had he been pelting at full steam?

The *happily-married-woman* calmly readjusted her position and turned to erudite his incongruous machinations much more closely...

She suddenly threw her glance over the Wool Exchange spiracle. His outrageous sentiment haunted the panels of hyaline as she crossed her *reindeer skins* back. Struggling in vain her eager will gradually waned below the wainscot. What a joint of steak!

A sickly spasm tied her stomach and her chamber flooded with Stilton. She scoured her pretty blue eyes once more as he defiantly inflated the blood vessels of his erectile tissue stimulated by their high altitude.

Her cool unblinking stars 'turned on' leapt to the top corner of her page and froze there, staring succinctly forward for a good deal of the journey. Her breast was in a turmoil. Snake fascinated, mesmerised.

Juliette could not unglue her charm even as he tonsured his pouting glanshead like the rope of a dried out prune.

He saw it every day and it never offended him! Her swollen thighs spontaneously parted as the waiter inferred her menu blowing hot and cold.

Her *iris* tottered round the walls to check she was the only voyeur dictating, but all was safe and well. She soon returned to measure with discretion the looming of his unshaded meat-bag.

Through each impassionable movement the dark land galvanised her to the base thing which flashed a greeting across the bleak horizon. A distinct aroma drifted from his peace-pipe.

As she bit on a hard solution the arrant knight demonstrated the shameless flaunting of his pikestaff without reserve.

216

"What do you do for a living?" asked the girls. "Are you a male model.."

"I'm a badminton coach!" snapped the Jellyman blithely..."Oh, him..I believe he's a...Singleman!" swivelling on his seat. "You'll have to ask him for yourself. I don't know anything about it...perhaps he's just a Jellyman."

"Actually, I'm an *itinerant pyrotechnologist*!" blushed F. They perlustrated blankly at him...and yawned. J. had no strongly held convictions.

But it soon came around to the traditional time for knocking the Iron Lady...even as the evening was thawing to a close.

Jelly was right on cue.
"Those bloody Tories!" he lamented. "Thatcher's Britain! They're all a toffy nosed bag of lousy 'gits.' Why don't they just load them all in the dog van and take them down to the river, after skinning them alive and making leather handbags from their callous crust. At least that way they could be put to some good use! Send the press into quarantine."

The general idea seemed to go down well, and he was rewarded with a fraternal pat on his uliginous back as he looked round smiling all the time. And it was quite permissable to use subliminal brain-washing.

"It's the old cow's birthday today," bleated the girl with Amazonian zeal. "What do you think we should buy her?"

"A ticket to Mars?" ejaculated the Jellyman immediately responding to her prompt.

"How about the Welsh windbag's roasted head on a platter with an apple to cork its mouth?" spanked the Flash. Had a Snowman suddenly entered the spot and left the door open? "Er, well, they all 'piss in the same pot anyway'..." he vacated.

J. said that if the GREAT DOME were to be overturned it could hold 3½ billion pints!

The midnight wanderers stepped into the great unknown. *Darth Vadar* led the route, but didn't seem to know where he was damn well going...F. wasn't sure if the woods were a safe place to loiter.

164

He had something to show her down on the pig-run. She was always stuffing her mouth with grubs so no wonder she was consistently riddled with worms.

Mathew collected all of them together, and began their mid-day banquet.

His mother felt cause for concern, but decided not to say anything since he was managing so peacefully.

Annabelle, Golliwog, Jemima, Raggy doll, and Teddy bear were each lovingly fed *cream and honey* by the sensitive young lad.

He lifted them soberly from the cardboard budgerow he had fashioned, and circumstantially attended their apparel in a manner which was totally blameless.

Browsing on the bristle doormat he tenderly brushed their unkempt filaments, administering to their every need and packing them neat in the box.

As the lemon flare sparkled serenely through the fecund hatchery, touching the brass plateframe, he smoothly cradled his special resolve swaying in his arms, before laying her down along the rail.

Mary froze in the threshold with the remains of the baking bowl oscillating in her fingers.

Suddenly, as if from nowhere, a black figure stood in the doorway, blocking the sunlight from his vision.

"He hadn't heard anyone clambering over the leather!" Danny's towering shape burgeoned on the step with his brawny nippers resting against the door reveal, the stink of the "Shoulder of Mutton" still reeking on his breath,..as Mathew, looking up, raised his hand instinctively to cover his face from the glare, and the man fired on him with spiteful venom.

Binkie had parted company long since! He stabbed the Woodbine on his shield. No chance licking the bowl out now! The clown had another think coming.

"What's this little *bastard* doing in *my house?*" he cried, swaggering to sequest his wife with mock astonishment. Then his pique settled on the comic muse caught napping.

19

at the pillar of the monatomic unit where the sentence was held in perennial execution. The two began to guffaw.

F. dimmed all the lights and turned the mirror against the wall. Strange the Inspector not mentioning his capture of the burgular, caught red-handed climbing a ladder through the booking office porthole...

With nothing better to do he flicked the switch of the circuit-phone, where the *Flapper* could gauge their gabbling non-stop until noon. He could easily discern the individual baritone clarity of the clones as they discussed the principles of car mechanics and the prospects for increased overtime.

Anus began criticizing the antics of the *kithless Wrecker* who had painted the whole establishment black as November. He had ended his destructive masterpiece with the salamander symbol of Aries, scrolled in rust over the burnished doorway, before smashing up the block bells and instruments with a crow-bar.

During the long hours spent in isolation *Angus Darke* had refused to turn the knob for any outside influences. Ever since his mother's recent demise the single tenant had become more and more withdrawn, culminating in his arrest on a minor shop-lifting charge which had triggered-off a severe bout of depression.

On the night of the tempest he had pulled-off for the last newspaper train before retiring down the treadway. A final cigarette as he sat resting on the rail bar in the moonlight was all he could muster to perk his spirits.

"So there he was!" chuckled Anus. "When I came up the steps he was lying at the side like a sack 'a dirty old spuds!"

"Bully should be alright for his *rest day* working now....his 'Box' must have really gone! I don't see why anyone should be lonely in this day and age."

The clan decided how best to carve up the spoils...
"I had a mate picked his nose once!"

57

He began to force the puppet into the wide open field, far more deliberately and daringly than ever before. Each deviant act re-inforcing his odd pathology. The student nurse quivered at the *operating table*...

She seemed desirous to discuss the need for common purpose, but our man had more pressing ideas to cope with. Too brief to form an attachment?

The passive eyes turned increasingly towards the brim of the book cover to face him, as they passed the huge phallic tower of 'King's Cross' with its immense masonic glans. To be honest their current relationship remained on the whole *rather* limited though.

Once again the deviant carried on the show for much longer than he need have. Her bleary buds eventually relaxed silently on the quintain and settled down to watch with rising adulation. Without another word she slowly followed the 'X' certificate, and cocked an eye sharply on his *thalamus*, although the plot was almost undecipherable, she gulped and regurgitated all her grub.(in an out 'a there!

His *utopian urge* buttered like a sunflower under the spray of saffron bleaching from behind the welt of cloud...he really must consider *circumcision*...the fulsome smell overcame the farmer's cram. His buttermilk rose to the surface. Blocks of stardust.

With the diesel coming gradually to a holt beneath the station canopy, filled with the summer primroses swinging rhythmically in their seasonal baskets of straw, the strange little man began ejaculating in syncopation with the application of the squeaking curb. The station master gloared with the watering can static in his grasp./j(O-nly 'jesturing!'

Suddenly he noticed Shittlegruber lurching on the bench with 'his' replacement.

The old *Lampman* was unable to contain his disgust. He turned to distract his colleague's attention. With his finger shaking nervously he pointed sheepishly toward a silver body laden in the azure firmament.

46

No matter how P. tried to stem his flow, untimely
times, he continued to spurt his oily spray around the
poached hulks, finally running out of canvas.
   While the chestnut mare hummed the Cutie Anthem he
attempted to disguise his extraneous seed. The odd-
jobber climbed down from his ladder and came to peer
with astonishment through the adjacent window. Then
sighing at his feet she even had the temerity to
importune him for his digits. Make believe.
   Pressing his muffit against the offending place P.
managed to make it to the gangway and perambulated
alongside the coaches of the seaside special.
   Camouflaging the magic drops of ambrosia in whose
potency and profit our very life depends the clockwork
fool loped mechanically along the distant platform to
the 'detention centre' of the pale green glasshouse
perched on the flange of the pier.
   A 'man-in-black' emerged from the sombre concourse.
"Who's that?" "The Signalman," of course.
   In the certain knowledge that he would be foregoing
his former ally on the down P. prayed for the hollow
earth to swallow him up. There was nothing about
Dorian a paper bag could not fix.
   Assaulted by the circumambience of electric hemlock
P. approached the other home with his zip still only at
half mast. If he tampered around the region further
people were liable to become suspicious.
   Once inside the den he had hours to contemplate the
homeward journey on witch to brandy his fertles. He
would just have to learn to be more patient.
   Through the looking glass flickering images of the
Mer-fuck rigadooned like shadows on the interior, but
Walt and his Hasas were nowhere to be seen.
   Anchored on a rock his eyes drained violently at the
scene. Every air hole in the stuffy cabin was highly
blocked. A fiction.
   P. alighted nimbly over the shining hum of Muses and
noted the brand new sailing diary adorned resplendently
at the bottom of the well-worn steps - a present from

The golden wedding ring on her prodder reminded him that her love was definitely not for permanent hire. Her mind jerked unerringly back to the lode-stone.

For the second time that afternoon the illusionist proudly exercised the new trick he had learned. There would never be a more desirable species of watch-dog... Look, no hands!

His penis exploded like a nuclear mushroom sending a generous amount of liquid splattering against the ceiling of the ward. For heavens at a bound the red hot geyser showered its slurry over all four walls of the speeding construction spurred on by the power of his will alone.

The coagulated syrup dripping from the newsprint gathered in its usual *Zuyder Zee*. The ends of his fingers seemed blown by a gentle puff of rime from the *dying star*. A cannon hole in the news.

The *heavenly body* brusquely detruded her breath. With a heave of dismay she relegated her gaze allowing him to laundress.

As he handed back the cloth ghost of a daily she vigilantly surveyed that the lid of his cellar had been sealed. She flushed but her drums remained muted.

So ripely rewarded, the Campaign Manager pulled out a purr of pleasure. "You're the kindest geezer I ever met."

It made a nice change to complete shooting *before* the glare of the hoofers.

As he stood in the queue at the exit Juliette stared apprehensively at the hump of his britches. A slobbering wen stretched directly across her eye level.

As the train chugged slowly to a stand she hastily scribbled him a note on her ringed expository.

When the rancorous passengers jostled for the door the charming journalist reached over and tugged him on the sleeve. She tore away the rejoiner with a sliver of shark floating in the draught of the gust.

Grinning inanely the proud Flasher emerged from the subway to skulk towards the ticket barrier. He shoved the correspondence in his coat and deliberately avoided her gape across the line.

john dillinger

"I'm a 'doctor-in-spite-of-myself,'" rippled the Flash. Pissed in the sty of 'Compostella.'

"I have no 'established' trends to defend and I refuse to belong to any recognised band. Consequently I have no-one to cushion the blow, and I do not allow another such probity to stick in the throat of my membership."

The bon-enfant-father-of-his-people paused.
"This is what I sincerely believe," he candidly postulated. Day of the 'Deathe.'

"You are far too serene for this tale of yours to be gospel so I am sure it is just a figment you have conjured up to succour your disagreeable tendencies."

"Are you masturbating at this moment?" he jeered.
"Beg pardon, but we are not in attendance for that sort of misdemeanour. I'm going to re-place the hand-set!"

The line went stone dead. F. turned with *hands of wood*. *Use it, don't lose it.*

"I don't want your lousy sympathy anyhow you fucking prat!" he stalled. *Nads fucking alley!*

He was completely disgusted with himself for lowering his sights in their direction.

What was so wrong with him that he had to go crawling with his tail between his legs to a Milesian?

Why couldn't he just blast himself out of their secular orbit by *true grit and determination?*

"*Fancy going on blind date?*"
Humanity in a nutshell!

THE GENEROUS 'Jock'
The Devil-doc
The Robbing Hood
The honest Archer
The soldier-poet
The doting deviant
The friendly fiend!

The cruel sea...

286

LINEKER

By nightfall she was fired from the string, so he locked the door in case she tried to sneak back while he was recuperating, placing a sign over the aboriginal; 'Strictly no admittance!'

At just after witching hour he extended his long refracting telescope, before the silvermoon expired.

Weaving its magic spell before plunging the planet once more into darkness the orb disappeared behind a scudding shade, and did not reappear until *housel*.

In the harsh March wind the girls huddled augustly together on the wooden bench. They trembled like kittens as he approached to discover ways of alleviating the tragic situation...

Camping out in only their sleeping bags on the hard terrain the little waifs had returned down the pasture from the mountainside, and had missed their last train home to Pendle. But as luck would have it the P.Way Pirates were out in force again and were smuggling their gear along the platform to the lighted grotto.

"What on earth are you doing here at this time of night?" asked the Signalman patter-eternally. He coaxed them up to the warm house; when the coast was clear he would phone for a taxi...he promised!

In the compound below Inspector Gilbert assembled the floodlighting for the 'Engineer's Possession.'

On the gallery bank his chrome dome dazzled everyone in sight by its reflective glare, until they moved the main operation to a mile distant from the points. Without looking where he was going he tripped over a signalling wire and fell flat on his face.

He slowly rose and made his way up to the Signalbox to sign over the line. After entering the cabin he dismantled his 'high visibility vest' and began to make friendly conversation with the garrison crew ensconced.

72

But the voyager had not yet reached his final port of call; 'Nosferatu!' wandered by the silken shards and admired the portrait of her recent atavist. He examined each intimate belonging before deciding with which close encounter he would like to convene his nuptuals.

The imminent pitch of dawn would still find him tending lovingly to her crinal curtains with the 'Snoopy' comb....the troublesome Snoopy alarm would still be waving its luminous limbs from the mantelpiece.

Before she mounted the scaffolding he would be chased away by the breaking of the 'making' spell.

The cat-burgular gave a disgruntled 'tut' 'tut' as he envisaged how he would respectfully remit the white door after his departure...

Mrs. Do-as-you-would-be-done-by, panting pathetically at his valance, would gently knock on his latch in the early morning streak.

If she was fortunate the old dutch might gain a peek of his hard-on; but only if he forgot to put on the bolt and pulled down his sheets like the best of all people.

A shiver ran down the Sleep-walker's spine as he wondered how long the debauched love affair could continue nose to tail. He stalled like an alabaster corpse...

Could no-one drive a merciful stake through his heart, and convert this shame to sadness?...and say, "Come on h-o-m-e, Mathew, all is forgiven!"

184

Perhaps he had imagined the girl, the compartment, the transvestite, and the Basque separatist?

With the shame of a shaman he loitered on the starboard side for times without number while the wadding tick-tocked down the stretch.

Aspiring for the restitution of his 'X' ray vision the *railwayman* could hear the shunter through the laminated bog glass as he noisily uncoupled the locomotive in two. But his mind was in a quagmire and he had drunk the last tango. Beast of the boulevards.

Only as the vehicle accelerated out of the station did the idiot finally saddle his hinny.

Secure in the bare supposition that he had probably preserved his nefarious freedom F. emerged from the W.C. and cracked his forehead in disgust.

As they began to gain speed he could clearly discern the rear portion of the express receding under the canopy...with his camera, his bucks, and every single one of his travel documents asking to be looted.

Poker-head turned to find everyone left on board frowning with conjecture in his direction.

Milked his freedom for all he was worth...!

> *'On swift sail, flaming.*
> *From storm and south.*
> *He comes, pale vampire,*
> *to my mouth...'*

His old ticker...

253

"Do you think he'll come in tonight?" he asked.
"I don't know," shivered Gretel. "They should be here soon though."

She began to sob with alarm underneath the sheets as she sucked her thumb against the lemon frayed blanket...Uncle Stan sucked his until he was twelve. By then it had withered away. It was just beginning to spit against the glass.

The rain started to lance more saliently, when they noticed the spooks clambering slowly up the pass. The Big-people were arguing about a man who had looked at her in the Shoulder. A car headlights dazzling the pattern hurried him back in the refuge.

Almost immediately he came creeping up the stairs, grinning wildly, with Mary snapping like empty thunder.

Her body bounced like a golf ball as it ricocheted down the steps to every steady thump of their heart.

"The 'Bogeymans' gonna getchya! The 'Bogeymans' coming up to getchya!" Danny jibed as he came staggering into their room clothed in ebony, and swiftly cracked on the switch.

The terrified beings vellicating in the swaddling pretended to be hard on.

Like a *private detective* he carefully inspected the bedroom carpet, feeling over the course woollen matress on his hands and knees with the expertise of a craftsman. Danny was up to his armpits in nicotine. The man in the moon had a gleam, and should have been fast asleep...

"Have you been out of bed, have you?" he screamed. "What did I tell you would happen if you ever disobeyed me again?" he stormed. "If you'd given them your tit he wouldn't suck his fucking thumb."

Danny reached instinctively for the hard metal strap with its axel of steel studs from the hook...and then he noticed the striking likeness

Meanwhile the pitcher was once more phoning his ma-in.
"Hello, it's only me," he said. "Has anybody said yet? I've been waiting hours for him," he whimpered. "This is the final straw. I'm not going to be messed around any longer." Could hardly run between two lamp-posts. He pushed his way through the crowd of the packed auditorium and prepared to start the swim without his missing adjutant. "It was definitely who you knew. Last weekend I was the cockswain in a ladies' regatta," muttered caterpillar. But there was a Black Swan look about her. Could she have been a secret agent. We are creatures of the flash!

He crossed his legs away from her solicitude with absolute clarity. Although T. had already missed his stop twice and had been acting rather outlandish to put it madly, she still helped him tie 'the spices with his bicycle, and carried his bodkin for him past the thicket snout. Heck he the power to prosecute!

"Do you always expose yourself to girls you meet on the train," she whined. "I do jobs you decide to go on the resort of the ice capped silver than where the disgusting grace of God makes..." "There but for the disgusting grace of God irlathlon was being held the competitors were already concluding a great twice around the atoll. Their next stage was a thirty-five mile cycle ride, and then they culminated with a still marathon.

A daymare shroud shuttled over the trees as the jellyman approached the edge of the water like a ripe cleaner's Captain Webb. "Always gonna be winners. I shivered hideously as he dipped his was in the ice-box. "It's cold as a frog," screeched a chap, returning to have a tome. Throws around him by his loving spouse. "Trunks made by 'B-d-pies'.

With iron-grit determination with across his brow the fundamental womanly leapt bravely into the log bank, and landed belly-flop in the drink, just inches in depth at that ebb on the sand. Dursey, dragging himself along the pebble strewn bottom the jellyman waded unobstructed into the invisory mist determined to get on with his downing." It that from a great height." could it have been an aeroplane.

"I think they look rather sweet," said F. "And you are intending to cure the sick?"

She revealed the snaffle between her red unchristened lips.

"I share a house with four other girls and a displaced lime-juicer. He loves the brown study!" she said. "They'll be meeting me at the barrier I hope. What time is it?"

As the conversation deepened the diceman toyed with the raffle of his fate. Should he or should he not? The uncertainty made his heart skip.

Removing the straw Dunstable from over his turgent crutch he blatantly examined her sylph-like hanger with consumate eclat. Her slim legs were covered in a layer of pink and lemon stripes. His mandible ached to paw inside her stonewashed shirt and manhandle her heaving fruits. His zoom lens extended closer...

"I'm so glad to have some good company on my journey round," she rippled. "These trips every weekend can be so boring"...his elbow cadenzaed toward the flint.

When he mined the seam Spike protested from his tawdry slumber. He 'stunk like skunk' but still managed to brag his *Pour le Merite* rawly at the altar.

Lo and behold his *dinnerjacket* had floated superfluously away at the Y.W.C.A. F. avoided the nosey Parker when she proceeded to ablutions.

Sarah shuffled her feet and decided to have a catnap. Then she searched for another activity to occupy her transient state in the corridoor of time.

"Would you like a browse through the Creature's Digest?" he asked. "I've already accredited the entire length of misdemeanours for you to appreciate."

"Thankyou," she smiled. "It's absolutely ages since I've scanned through one of these." She turned anti-clockwise and crossed her athletic frame away from the landscape.

Discarding his useless dodge the dilettante pruned his peeling prepuce to weld a solid ring.

323

RASPUTIN

It was true that some of them would never question the compulsory daily worship.
And naturally assumed that one set of values were *the good* and any other belief *contrary to the good*.
The 'non-believer' would burn for *ever and ever and ever* he assured them. Grinding his teeth unmercifully he shaped his clasp into a steeple and evangelized *glad tidings* of Tartarus.
'Inside each and every one of us we have a glowing white orb which is called the soul, whose original sin is washed away by the sacrament of Holy Baptism, and whose only stains are caused by the committing of venial, or Mortal sin, this latter Mortal sin being the cleft palate of evil corruption.'
That there were strict codes of moral discipline and social behaviour they should follow pedantically, but that it didn't really matter being ignorant of the complex ideas involved (in the faith of transubstantiation;) to enter through the propylon of Heaven all individuals must, of necessity, become as a 'child in heart,' it transpired. The number of Commandments were ten. 'Honour thy father and mother' et cetera, et cetera.
To christen his crowning glory only the most exemplary of the little girls were allowed to dust his dorp at lunch-time, and administrate a few extra chores that needed straightening round his private area. Gretel was one of the 'chosen few;' for which a bag of jelly-babies seemed suitable reward for her services. He had a housekeeper suffering from *elephantisis* who stuck her bowl at the Dog and gun - conveniently it transpired.
The corpulent Canon in his black lead smock continued with his sermon at the top of his iron throat. As he enthused about the 'immaculate conception' he reached a fever pitch of ecstasy, his synchronizing blob coloured sharply in alternate hues of 'fire and brimstone' boiled over with images of Satan carnal. How the Senate lay back on scented couches until they spewed their guts up...

28

"Life's too short," he said...and melted into thin air.

Beside the garden shed he could see Alice-Eva frying their muck through the murky diaphane. He could auscultate her muffled recitation of 'the Captain of the Buffs.' It was a favourite stand-up piece when her squaddies resided at barracks in the *cultural capital of Guardhouse*. Had a pair of drawers they used as an 'out-rigger.' Always had her curlers in.
As she packed the razor-edged weapons into bread-and-butter sandwiches her flesh obscenely swagged from the ripples of subcutaneous waste.
The walls were thick with grime and several skins of paper jockeyed for position at the skirting board. They must have had the dust shipped-in especially from the Luggins. Pus-bag crunched a slice of gristle in between their legs. The lop-sided jaw of the floor was iron-clad with crustaceans. If you'd accidentally spilled some blow-bubble it would have left a dewy patch on the fringe.
Her corpulent 'washer-woman's' cheeks flushed with mauve as she discerned who had dripped in for a whirl. The many faces dropped, but she decided to take her time anyway...and she usually rushed to make a fuss.
"He's here again look!" she loosely mumbled and glared distrustfully at her husband.
"I wish you wouldn't keep encouraging him. Doesn't he have any friends of his own age?"
When the dartsman turned the clavis his grandson floundered on the brink...the slob pretended to jump back in fright as if she'd seen a duffy, although the boarding had been pre-arranged.
She tossed the pillowcases carelessly to one side and wouldn't look at him. Ogger still had that clothes peg stuck to his jersey. He had once been swept from the riverbank by a marauding troupe of rodents. Stung by a mosquito on his backside once as well.
"He scares the living daylights out of me!" she whimpered morosely feigning a cold shiver down her deleterious spine. Something wrong with his sugar; he drinks fizzy pop! Canyons scalded into his skin.

68

He paused for breath and adjusted his quare nippers. "I've been talking to a chick from the homeground who used to have the low-down with you," he sniggered.
"Her boyfriend chains her bare arse to the blistering red hot radiator and screws the hell out of her! She swears that you were a scruffy little eel at kindergarten." All shook up!
"She couldn't believe me when I informed her how much you had burst at the seams. It's a pity she's no babe." Vassal miscreant! Edge of the known galaxy.
"I've had that recurring dream again!"
He giggled just like 'Willie Carson' riding a flea.
"I dreamt that I was just a shiftless, spineless *Jellyman* without any real backbone at all in me... and that without my complete works of prestidigitation I wouldn't even appear capable of far-sighted folly, or voluntary euthanasia. World's so full of shit man."
But it was always difficult to discern if Bates was just manoeuvering one of his many sides, and he had already rebuked the *hoi polloi* more than once for being too afraid to fib. Mental detecting. *Beings* were unemployable! Givers or Takers. Which one are you?

The Cock-or-two repeated his story several times and offered his 'screwed-up' sketch of 'Lucretia Borgia' with a penis lodged in its cochlea. Once had a brush with the law. What's hot on the catwalk Tophat?
They discussed the gouache water colour which someone had presented as part of their final exhibition; a gnostic metaphor containing an *Oran Utan* being fellated by a member of the 'Tuatha' as it hung on the cross at Calvary. Only the good die young!
Underneath its horrid caption, 'Suffer me to come onto little children;' obviously a biblical allusion regarding the sacrificial crucifixion and entering into heaven. *Shunga*...no black without white.
Its effect on the evangelical movement at the college had been diabolical. Sins of the flesh! Below the salt. Must have gone through a fortune in tracing-paper conscientiously objecting. Defended his intellectual property throughout.

244

Here is the letter I've been meaning to send you,
meaning to send you for such a long time now.
I know when you read it, I may be dead...
I may be dead for such a long time now.
But read it, I know that you will one day!

Do you remember when I carried you quite far?
I was loaded with scales but did not think twice,
Oh, what a pretty girl always to me!
I felt very tender, I only felt tender,
and penned the way some porters do...

If ever I hurt you, which I know was not seldom,
then you'd climb and come round with the tide.
From *Whitecastles* I swung you, and sweetly embraced you,
forever I hoped this would be!
But then I grew serious, and you frowned with sad
Autumns, though I should, I never quite understood why...

But there's something quite often, I meant to beseech you,
which tossed like a leaf in my mind.
Will you quite often, or just for a moment...
will you please *be my bride*,
will you please *be my bride*?

Though I once left you, to shelter your secrets,
and for once march on alone with your cares,
You never quite left me, you never deserted me,
if I could, I'd just like to explain;
I loved you, I love you, I always adored you,
and think of you where ever I glide.

Justice has been done.

"Only jealous!" hissed the Infanta.

242

"Personally I don't care what they do in private, as long as they don't scare the horses."
She showed him the door. Tiny bit camera shy. Set off like a six year old looking for his sock.
He pulled the camera strap over the shoulder of his leather bomber jacket and wanted to hug her so much that he thought of nothing else...knocked the stuffing right out of him.
When he sat down in the queue the licence dodger eventually gave breath. It was like watching the formation of a snow crystal through a microscope. His pulse seemed to quicken.
"Press Photographer?" he asked, nodding at the Pentax.
"Only for the 'News of the World!'" soft-pedalled Mathew.
Just before dinner time the snapshotting dude was summoned into number 6 court as the final entrant in their group.
With his dome flapping like a ragged patchwork quilt the ugly monstrosity loped like a squiffy mechanism. His heart in a silvery cage. Rood-loft.
He entered the wooden pulpit beside the pews to strut and fret his hour upon the planks. Blushing to be encountered with a cloud. She howled like a bitch bringing herself off.
Once again he was staggered by the extravagant luxury of the proscenium arch which paled all other dressings into insignificance.
This grossly obnoxious farce unwound with unmitigated opulence. Step into line! She showed him the door! Choose who she bloody well wants.
The usher who had been making such pleasant conversation quickly averted her eyes.
"That you did openly, lewdly, and indecently, with intent to harrow the anvil, expose your erect *penis* outside her Riding Stables....." contrary to the *vagrancy* act of 18...something or other.
Thank the lucky stars. Once again the chamber was free of blasted reporters. Retracting his Sigma.

He left the quacks on Church street with his prescription and trotted through the yard along the crowded shopping precinct to the *Apothecary*. He ducked in an alleyway when he saw Moran halting down the hill.
The attender was a beautiful girl with blonde hair who smiled at him as he glowed like a morning lantern.
On Saturday there were at least six assistants working behind the counter as he handed in his note.
His cream dome perspired like a windscreen as he appeared to be examining a shaving stick.
They each took it in turns to examine the contents on the pad. "Do you know what this is used for?" they giggled. "We've never heard of that brand before."
Flash explained once again that *Supersod permanent lawn replacement* was a new 'wonder drug' from the States which was supposed to cure his congenital /deformity?
To prove his point he held up the advert which Esmerelda mark 2 had recently posted.
But they didn't seem to click on...until customers began surveying his summit in the queue.
His face began blistering as Moran gandered against the door-glass.
After six months of pate-wetting the villi hair had still not begun to show signs of curding.
F. sheltered nervously beside the stack of featherlite while the senior chemist answered on the fax. "You'll have to wait one moment!"
Behind the counter *Amini* touched her up. She glared obnoxiously toward the hairless article. What a bloody cheek! Who on earth wants to hear from you!
The red-head passed him a mystery bag containing the magic lotion with a solemn expression as he dispensed ninety pounds cash into their till.
The other hosts loitered curiously over his scalp. As he reached the door the entire staff burst out laughing in giltish titters.

Gliding lugubriously by the supervisor's mess the bedraggled Flash was just about to slink down to the sidings when he heard a familiar voice ring-out from the sentry catch.
"Hey there, *Bald Eagle!*"
"What the hell are you doing down in this neck of the woods?" vituperated the 'Flying D.'
His wild expression gradually subsided to a calmer ocean.
"Visiting relatives," he gulped. "Did you earwig about Katie's initial suttee?"

====================================

The 'subdued' 'Flash!' taking the bread, and broke it and said. "Take this and eat; this is my body!"
'How do you hold a 'moonbeam' in your hand?'
Parting is such sweet sorrow...
He finally got his '*end-away*.'

The copy-cat filler smeared her super-sternal crotch!

"I love you, I love you, but the world grew too hot!"

"He'll never go to heaven now! You know it's a SIN to look at girls!"

"Oh, he'll get over it!"

Seemed a bit short for breath though...

If a small fish wants to survive it has to tell the *fisherman* where the big fish are hiding.

But it's later than you think my friend...that was very pusillanimous of you.

Dick *Ebola* spyed in her bedroom!

====================================

She noctambulated his plodding back to his filth for the second conjuncture. He helped himself to the residue of gulp having given up the ghost...

"Look at the beautiful scenery you've been missing," he diced. "The sway is like *Quicksilver* and the sky is like silk." With Canute's hands to whip up a storm.

But she hardly spoke another word. Was it something she had consumed or had he put the cart before the horse? Played left-back for England!

After tracing Pisa he deserted the empty compartment and deviated down the catenation to condone his compulsive habit. Unable to forage in palladium he fell into a deep slumber upon the bench.

Suddenly there was a gust of cold wind. The door blew open in an avalanche. Grenadiering in the gap tottered a slimey creature from the hills.

The lofty 'Mountain man' was dressed in a kilt of Yeti skin trimmed with fur gaskins.

A horrid stench rattled from wall to wall as he slid the screen across the passage...

F. woke to find the brute stretched across the other side. Flames of the window above me.

As he quickly gathered his belongings the Darkman seemed to floe his breath.

F. redeemed himself another quod at the front of the plummeting tumbrel.

It was daylight as they trammelled through the overcast countryside when the lid of the compartment drifted wide once again.

A giant hoof stepped inside the room and found a seat crushed in the middle of Tuscany.

Rubbing his grumbling abdomen the leviathan began lacerating an enormous can of corned beef with a penknife from his rucksack.

Sweat was pouring from his ruddy flesh and a pungent odour permeated from his guts as he chomped his cob of bread in syncopation. His soporific globs seemed to barm into viscous broth.

One traveller actually held a scarf to their nose. A local woman muttered disagreeably. He grunted a brief reply in a voice which was *just as awful*.

244

While the full moon drifted above the jagged mountain slopes a whirl of mist hovered outside the cabin. As if by magic the dragon slithered from his craterless pit. A peculiar argent fog seemed to surround his steaming fresco, bottled in Montgomery's beret.

The midnight necrophiliac with the talcum mask of white flew within firing range of her cruising lozenge.

With supersonic energy Grendel 'Big Sug' was suddenly crouching naked above the dozing aristocrat flashing his hirsute penis at the reedy.

They say that 'gentle-men prefer blondes,' but this 'Nosferatii' was a bugger for changing his mind.

Little 'Eva' was far too drab. Her huge gun tube was puckered and distorted. At this ungodly hour of the pendulum his reptilian tongue slurped inside the chasm of her lips. Her windows of breath.

By the light of the silver moon which pranced over his achromatic scales he slid his sly penis over the mile long lane of her muttering acoustics.

Would she ever have the power to escape his coprolite clutches?

Grendel 'grease lightening' pitched his sleeping bag blindly to one side and his eyes blinked from the intense concentration which the lunar period demanded.

The motion picture bowled along like frames in an early monochrome. Until the cartoon gradually sharpened...and froze in the Projector's wheel. His automatic lens snapped her palpable cognizance in solid kamikaze technicolour.

Looming to his full height the naked ape motored his leaning tower to buttress on her orifice. To his complete astonishment Heidi suddenly lifted her head and began muttering in *Hindi*.

She remained absolutely stiff but was alerted by the sudden bolt. Anything to declare?

Heidi lifted the cover up to her mouth and scrutinized the space to see if the beast would encore...sure enough his apparition slowly rose from her feet and stooped across the pulsing crypt.

243

'Good grief,' erudited the Flash.
An edition of the *Guardian* was held upside-down in his gripe.

F. scurried past the ice-cream salesman and covered his tracks behind a marl until he melted into thin air.

The Goliath tramped round the piazza into the city with the tiny rucksack perched on the base of his firline.

F. headed in the opposite direction, and immediately peeled off his britches to sunbathe within a stones' throw of S.M.Degli Angeli.

His pin-money was soon being dissipated on a gallon of liquid squash.

As the locals urinated in a cranny of the ancient mortar a large contingent of *Wops* gathered on the turf not far from where he was swooning.

From the grassland nearby somebody wolf-whistled...one of the bunch blew him kisses.

There it was again! He pretended not to have noticed. It suddenly dawned on him that the traffic was coming to a stand at the lights. Lower the sun-glasses.

Suddenly two tall men in blue emerged from a squad car parked alongside the rank. They strode toward the naked torso hurriedly retrieving his dignity.

"Put your shirt on at once!" he dictated in pidgin English. And then..."What do you think this is...a beach?" Flipping *braggatoni*!

From the metropolis he veered toward the nocturnal fringes on the sequel.

The strawberry blonde '*Courier*' must have considered it an honour to be so enlightened in this manner.

Although she had the most to gain by his *public exposure* he certainly wasn't going to empty his balls for her! But she soon grew bored of his blustering sabre-tooth rattling. He stood on the brink.

As the bustling market blistered past the furtive *Flash* fiddled with his foreskin, and juggled his richly baked almonds bursting with developing fluid.

245

"I do love you," she howled. "I couldn't possibly love you more than I already do."

"Please don't let anything go wrong with us," she begged him. "I don't think I could stand another broken relationship."

The *Aphrodite* from the 'Terminus' came to wait in the stall beside him. Gertrude rushed to throw her arms around his neck and vomitted over his vestment.

The high speed locomotive shivered out of the platform, but she did not reappear to refresh the parts other beers cannot reich. Eva had been abandoned in the restaurant car when the unit split in half. Only by swimming with the tide was she able to rejoin them at Melun. Viva Espania!

"Well, I did warn you!" grinned the Flash. He was becoming something of an expert in these matters.

They toasted a glass of *Bordeaux* to celebrate her amazing recovery to the Silver Streak.

Her unaccompanied luggage was still standing in the corner of the compartment as they strayed toward the dark bewilderment at a considerable rate of knots.

The two cousins had spent the season squatting in the *Citadel* with aboriginals before their hair-raising escapade.

He offered to sketch their portraits with his pencil...which he recorded in the '*Priapus*,' as they passed through the higher firs, and entered the snowline chugging at a regular rhythm.

With malice aforethought F. volunteered to kip down on the floor between them.

If only he could lay the matter to rest? Lullabied by their homophonous sound he prepared to strike a low third. Heidi shifted her tease in his direction. He discarded his useless down-at-heels and prepared for the *time of change*...

242

DO NOT INTERFERE WITH MY PHONE CALLS (September 2017)

Overheard ma talking to the Agency this morning. The Church Warden said she could find what she was looking for at Roy's of Wroxham. "But how will I get there?" she asked.

"I could run you there like I used to do!" I suggested. "The car is only up the road…"

"Oh, will you shut up!" she screamed. "Why haven't you found somewhere to live yet?"

When I came back home there was a note waiting for me:

'DO NOT INTERFERE WITH MY PHONE CALLS. YOU HAVE A BAD ENOUGH NAME IN THE VILLAGE!'

- ✓ Supported by all members of the family
- ✓ Charming and talkative in the right company
- ✓ Complained I was cramping her style
- ✓ Only had myself to blame for everything
- ✓ Good at stabbing you in the back and telling lies
- ✓ Popular with everyone on the third row

Mum was laughing when I got home; she'd hidden all the keys again.

With a white-fanged smile he veered towards the youngest of his entourage flashing his hirsute penis and prodding the beast against her ivison prow.

As he gently lifted the brim of Vanessa's bright throat from her wallet the still shimmer of a crucifix revealed itself falling from her path. Her hithered eyes ogled instinctively, watching him carefully where he had ruminated to a safe distance.

Grendel motioned moodily around the hull for a pliable well-wisher who would indulge themselves in his milk of heathen kindness.

She was sinking deeper into the coma he had woven with his indirect influence. He checked to see if the ruby chalice was still spotless.

Millicent had a beautiful tassel of long red hair spilling over the margin of her labia. A lush wide mouth which contrasted her kite like frame was gore with a hedge of tiger blood.

The "ne'er been had" stirred restlessly in her troubled repose. Even Grendel felt a chord of pity strike his heart when he recalled her sad necrology.

White faces lay filled with the rich bouquet of life tilted her busy legs gateways to forty-five degrees and dangled her jingling arm unconsciously over the cushion, twitching spasmodically as she mumbled deliriously in her night dreams.

A dark shadow moved outside the contours of the lighthouse. The figure went unnoticed as the shutter bent even nearer and slid his partbuckle along the length of her labial phonograph.

Her arm jerked like a crane and a frown exasperated across her brow as the throbbing purple of his ruddy whip prexied ever tighten into the vision recess of its toy. Once more jarring against her pretty white bur with the bloated outer vessels of his conch shell pinched. Happy as a pig in a poor-door-file ring.

Through prunes and prisms the pregnant savient propelled rhythmically against her humping head, supporting his cramping effort with an arm on terrafirma, and jowling against her soft pink cheek

"But I was born like a shoat in the rain. If only I could turn over a new leaf. Where has my sweet Proserpine flown?"

F. could discern the *maggot whisper*. A brief shrill falsetto as the Martian held his knob over the mouthpiece. A politically correct form of castration.

"Er, just how long have you been wedded to this strange vernacular? It sounds as if you have fallen into a terrible morass, and a potentially damaging cartusion is developing. Are you under a Medical man?" he floundered. Presented a wide back.

"About fifteen years," confided the Flash. "Ever since I was at pubic school...is that protracted enough for you? Pissed in the tomb of Rameses II."

"On how many occasions in your estimation?"

"There must be thousands."

"I'm absolutely horrified!" he whistled. "Do you behave indecently wherever you deviate?"

"I've gutter-crawled my way over many borderlines," boasted F. "But I've not usually creamed with anyone I've known since kindergarten."

"I've acted rudely in the Strangers' gallery, and the waxwork museum...I splattered my load over the tiles of St. Pauls."

"I've done it in the arch of 'Glastonbury Tor,' and satisfied my gratification from 'R. Soles to 'John O'Groats.'"

"I was even stimulating myself at the fag-end of the street when the minster was struck by a hand of extra-atmospheric tension. There isn't a gaslamp in the eastern sector where I haven't trifled or a darkened alley-way where I haven't wondered."

"Storm-trooping toward every tunnel that held an opening I've traipsed to the bull's eye of Highway 61'!."

"And I've rejected the data contained in the psychology of addiction, and elucidated the subsequent principles :-

"You've a very *'bad attitude,'*" chanted the Martian verbosely. "It will serve you very well right. Do you think that you will scamp again...soon?"

Of course F. could not give him a guarantee.

"Surely we work to live, not the other way around? Man does not prosper by bread alone...I just want the chicks to look up to me, preferably in a kneeling position."

"Is there anything which will turn the tables?"

"When the earth is flooded with my seed!"

"Why should a male administrator like yourself assist me to compete on equal terms? I've already tripped through a barren terrain of myth. Have you ever had a faggot of Hyrcynian wood shoved up your arse?" Male. why should you?

"We're not here to discuss my logogriph!" hissed the Martian sternly. "Is it purely *sexual frustration*? Or are you singularily too lazy to rudder a stable relationship to a wench of your own disposition? You're certainly deranged!" insisted the clansman. "Do you think that you will ever *commit rape*?...I mean...have you ever considered suicide as a more honourable option?"

"The thought of suicide is a powerful solace; by means of it one gets through many a tough night," wobbled the Flash. "The familiarity of the superior embitters because it may not be returned...we are punished most often for our virtues."

The Martian stared down at his dial.

"Did you ever grease the palm of a *hooker*? Some of us are destined to scan the heights," he mused, "while others are content to forage in the filthy gutter."

"I'm an *'aids-free-zone,'*" repulsed the Flash. "If safer-sex doesn't luge any permanent waters of bitterness in this age of increased *sexual tolerance*. My term of art is the jewelled handle of *no-love*, I have no port of call."

"Just what species of queer fish are you?" he mauled. "They ought to pox you in a flipping stink-tank!"

Janis asked if there would there be a fruitful outcome to their union.

The Oracle replied with terrible accuracy; she would 'fall into a bottomless pit for all eternity'...the woman reacted with an incantation of her own.

Was 'La Papillon' chimera, or simply masquerading as one of the 'lost tribe?' He rightly guessed the awful truth; her soul was *black* and her motives riddled with devious corruption.

The opponent suddenly decided on a rip-tide of watershoot. Unzipping her nylon she deliberately left the door open and pulled the coy Flasher inside. Janis flung the shower curtain wide attempting to expose him to the buck private.

"Look at her face!" urged the conspirator. "She has an inkling what we are doing." But F. refused to give them ammunition...Were they all going up the wall?

With the lighting turned down the misbegotten crump hid in the dead of night while they cavorted together on the mish-mash.

Janis *Littlewhite* guided his mawler into the wide recesses of her honeypot. It was certainly similar to a 'paper-hanger's bucket...,' but her cunt had molars.

He stood over the woman's head, but she resisted. Becoming angry when he pushed her demonstratively on him, and refused to do him homage.

"What do you think I am?" she asked. "Why don't you grease the palm of a call-girl if that is all you want."

She rammed him into her prurient frame stripped to the bone just as the next door neighbour arrived in the corridor to fiddle with his clavis.

"Please don't rend me by inches!" she screamed at the top of her voice..."You must tell me how much you love me!" And like an idiot he did. Her multiple orgasm flowed around him like a scalding flow of lava. She bucked like a livewire.

"Do you always have this effect on women?" she asked him.

"Are you certain of your facts?" he asked. A cold finger seemed to scratch down his spine and he gulped to bridge his scepticism.

"It's the vile revived corpse of a fallen angel," she confirmed.

"Somebody you've crossed swords with the day before yesterday...and you're going to sell your useless sportscar to buy me an engagement ring," she added.

F. was downtrodden by a stampede of spectral horses. Even Hammer horror films made him sleep with the lights on. He tried to be objective and explain it by means of her suspect mentality. The glass goblets in her cabinet shivered like a house of cards.

"What do you see when you look at me?" he asked pensively, trying to change the point of emphasis.

She fastened her coven eyes directly on the trapped *animal soul* of the *Wickerman*..."First there's wood, then there's paper, then there's stone!" she fizzed.

Suddenly she froze and spun away.

"Don't!" she said. "Don't look at me!" Dropping her gaze to the limit.

A prior personage had commanded her to avaunt.

"His face is like *the King of the Jungle*!" she imparted. "He crouches with his right hand upon your shoulder and his growls chill me to the very bone."

"That's my ascending sign," he paled. "Can you tell me more?"

She shook her head. "It's a ghastly breed. I cannot look!" she confessed.

"Tell it to go away or I cannot continue." A strange half smile rewarded on her summit.

A tremendous boom screamed from within the very brick of her tabernacle. It sounded like the clanging of heating pipes. Ultra-violent.

"What the hell was that?" quivered the *Flash*. The sound nearly made him jump out of his skin. His eyes began watering and his pulse rate quickened. He felt himself shaking and sweat was pouring down his emaciated mane. Offered him a black coffee.

HAPPY AS A PIG IN SHITE AGAIN

The old Lampman's bottomless black wells cradled upwards towards the latrine rim of the silver wheel, and called for another implement to be borrowed from the nearby mob.

"Go see if they have a spare..." he begged.

The door was ajar to their open cess pool so he cautiously entered the Den-of-lazy-bones.

Dregs and dottle were scattered around the huge oak benches of their cabin bartalling their gambolling caper.

A stale stench from the Fatman's obese hull fouled the rancid air with its reeking perfume as he traipsed across the clinkered ground of their 'fleapit.'

The sudden activity caused some of the workers to stir their heavy eyelids and fribble from their cat-nap. This hut of ill repute could certainly have done with a squirt from that well known brand of *cleaning fluid*: The waters of *Lethe*.

A hazy cloud of smoke rose up from Alec's pipe and obstructed the passage of light as Flash stumbled like the *waiter on Providence*.

With his 'parker' pulled tight over his head, and a boyish bloom upon his weary face, he hesitated on the border of the orlop deck.

A host of malodorous men omniverously callipered his form as he stammered for a spare 'screwdriver.' He could feel the eyes of *Ludlam's beast* eating into his flesh with a copulatory gaze.

Suddenly their Crow-haired-young-ganger emerged from the greasy secluded kitchen where he had been hawking the stranger, as he wavered self-consciously in the hornet of the smoking-room. A flame still burnt upon the filthy nigger stove.

At first glance F. did not twig the waggery.

"I've only got the one!" smirked *Tarbuck* facetiously, as he tossed his semi-erect penis... "but it's a wee bit blunt I'm afraid."

From the open grassland Flashman chased the Lampman into the soot secluded cloisters, brandishing the

In a moment of *divine inspiration* he succeeded in holding the ring around his iron lantern, and mocked her ghoulish interest with a multitude of rhythms. Her ecstatic eyes fogged with snow as the pervert's erection grew. Like a gnarled rod the impoverished penis faintly smiled and made her shiver.

A feeling of complete nausia bourned like simmering midnight as he sickly contemplated reaching *rocket launch*. He vowed that on the next occasion he would not wear any such encumberances.

The sight of her goose-pimpled thighs made his heart race faster. She had matured considerably since the Grammar School where she had been captain of that winning netball team.

The lids of the surprised *sightseer* opened and closed like a pair of drafty shutters as he initiated a further late edition of his *daring auxiliary supplement*.

Her heaving boobs drooped over the couch exposing her brassiere line near the deserted moss of the Peace Hall.

With each new fifth her face grew increasingly cadmium. *The favourite's* concern managed to manifest itself on the gleaming glans with obvious guilty feelings and ambition.

Should he or shouldn't he if that was what she really desired? Bring herself to climax...bring himself to climax? - In a public place? Why, that's indecent!

Her dreamy eyes lustfully melted over and an uncontrolled dribble of saliva trickled from her gum shield, as she deliberately placed her magazine on the rack so that she could suck his brains without anymore bothersome distractions.

There was a lingering doubt that something could be out-of-step though.

The sand of the egg-timer shuttered towards a showdown. The destination station quickly approached on the horizon, as the *figure-head* hummed intensely to his loathsome mesmeric tune.

"It was only a 'flash in the pan,'" he grinned.
For the first time in the witness box F. noticed the inkling of a smile sneaking across Stalker's Sunderland carriage.
The Union official bleated desperately on F.'s behalf. He even managed to include that they had attended the same primary school.
"Look, it's a fair cop, guv!" he abjured. "What about another slap on the wrists...have an ounce of pity or nobody else will have him on their books," he begged.
"Give him one last chance to put the record straight. You have his word that he will strive to keep his nose clean."
"None of my concern," sniffed the *Generalissimo* aloofly. "But thankyou for your protracted plea of mercy," he smirked.
"However we must *increase* his previous light sentence. After a discussion with my counterpart I am prepared to show a *dan-diprat* of clemency."
"For the buffeting he will be reduced in grade to 'Railperson.' I am not into gossip mongering," he gleamed. "I'm not prepared to alter my decision in any way whatsoever," he scorched. "Take it or leave it. I have other urgent business to attend to."
Stalker made it clear the hearing had expired its sunny-side and that his contentions were strictly 'off the record,' and totally irrelevant.
The Area-manager was growing hot under the collar when F. rose to speak up for himself at last.
He presented the panel with a list of the occassions when *extra-terrestrials* had onerously omitted a T.R. entry. He said that although old Geordie had only recently retired, so there was no possibility of him being implicated, as far as he knew the trains concerned were not still parked on the main line holding up the other traffic.
"There are more than fifty similar instances which have not been seriously scrutinised. Why can the *aliens* pass the buck when drivers pass through *red lights*, while I am punished severely for minor discrepancies?"

222

He peeled his giant foreskin over only a quarter of his cupola and danced a turkey-trot along the splashboard.
"When the cat's away," he whistled, and entered the quad in a crack.
The *flower of pink* gazing up from the floor jumped with fright but her vocal chords still remained muzzled with shock. With the hockey stick in his grip he offered to toss her for a bout of greasy pole. Sarah's eyes began to pop at the exalted one's horn. She could almost crib the futhorc on his arrow-head.
As he leant to confer the wet sponge on her outstretched palm his erect penis sprang from its hood like a 'Jack in a box.' The purple head shone healthily from the shaggy pile below his shirt. His knob glistened under the light of her response.
Kneeling just inches away from his 'Spanish eye' the girl dabbed at the carpet to mop the overflow.
Intent on knuckling down to the task she edged discretely closer to his cusp. The finer strands of her ash blonde hair became stuck to the surface of his throbbing glans. He nudged his turgent organ against her bright auricular shank. Go for it! In for a penny, in for a pound! Drench of the Sugarplum dairy.
Sarah contemplated humbly at his feet but did not pay further lip service to his masterclass. He could hear Mary calling at the bottom of the ravine, and that was enough to make anyone feel more docile.
"This rag needs wringing out," she sniffed, devoid of histrionics.
He decided to align himself better so that her blue balls could no longer ignore his cantharides.
She hovered in all directions round his bloated cam and seemed happy to forecast when it might hail. She still didn't say a dickie bird about his multicoloured braces, but blurted on the way home!
In a matter of seconds he could have secreted his fluid and then he would have been out of harness, but M. began to chase up the stairs as if the building had been seared, so he novated to jack-in his deal.
"Good lass Sa-Sa!" he felicitated. "A merry Christmas and a very happy new year to you all."

209

"I've always thought there was something funny about me," gleamed F.
"If found guilty you will expect to be dismissed from our service."
"Until that point you are to be transferred to work as a 'carriage cleaner' in the sidings with a stipulation that you are segregated from any contact with women."
"Because of your position you are a risk and danger to the public. You will report to the timekeeper dead on nine o'clock tomorrow morning."
"It's against all the rules!" they hailed in unison.
F. felt almost ecstatic. So this was the toe of the rainbow. Now he could finally let his hair down? Should he rush forward to shake them tirelessly by the hand throwing his shoddy arms around their necks? I don't like 'Tuesdays.' Penis-man!
With a preternatural lack of self-respect the unnatural Flash departed the ghost haired geriatrics in the brumal little penitentiary which housed the southern mutants.
Then walked calmly into their office next door to book his remaining annual leave. With the gift of celibacy to hand. Like a withered oak...
'I am a diversifying personality,' said F.
When he docked at the home depot having conducted his diagram for the day F. was ambushed by the Union man who demanded to know why his name had been mysteriously erased from the rosters. F. was clutching his side...had there been a knife wound?- Astrophobia
Even Gerry Archer turned his back on him. Could there have been an outbreak of *buebonic plague*? Six bowls of sugarlumps. Professional funny-man.
"I suppose at your age it's the only way of attracting attention."
"What's going on Tufty?" remitted the genial fellow. "Why can't you tell me the details of your interview? They can't just suspend you from your normal duties without prior notification or a formal discipline."
"I'd really like to help if at all possible."
"Too sad!" sobbed the Flasher, but it was too late to cry.

338

To stop the gap he reached for the bottle of *Lambrusco*. Prizing her two mutton legs apart and holding her ankles F. healed the torrent with a kick from the heel of his boot. E' gone mad, Ladykiller!
It was the best days work he'd ever done...
The knight errant placed the diadem of oak leaves on the mound of her bio-degradable monticle as he glanced in the mirror and began to suck his thumb contentedly...where was Gretel?
His brow was beaten with flour as he reached *touchdown beneath Estel Negre*. Here were the bald facts of his case. Ma'am! Shut the fuck up!
The Milesian bobbed in the cock-pit to thrum the first three notes of Mozart's requiem. The fat-lady sang. A desolate gas-station of the suburbs.
It even seemed anamorphic. How very sick. Dipped in red ink he crayoned an outline of the Madonna on her cheek. There was a light at the end of the tunnel. He sucked out her brain with a straw, lit a candle inside and swung it on a chain. If he consumed her belongings would it act like a tonic?
With his worn-out cranking handle he removed a lavender from the real exhibit and tossed it carelessly in the argon humming with *castratos*. It was a Capital Punishment. He seemed to be walking on the *Mare Nubium* or in the far depths of a supernova.
For the first time in years he could dissolve the pangs... Word Architect. Every dog had its day! And the stars of heaven fell down to earth as of a tree shaken by a mighty wind. She vanished like a summer fall. Education, Education, Education!
He felt like a new man. Guilty of an act he did not commit. And god bless all who sail in her...
Hail Caesar! Those who are about to die salute you... 'fell over-board'
For the angel of death, purification is at hand... sharpening his weapon.

For these are the words of 'LANDRU!'
Just a poor 'Word-Wizard' afterall that!

343

"Don't your Inspectors ever check the registers except when I'm on duty? Why is there always damage to the Signalbox apparatus after each shift that *the Spiv* has been in harness?"

The Mayor screamed and packed his briefcase. "How dare you try to tell me how to operate the schedules!" he barked dogmatically. "It's not the position of subordinates to go beyond their stations." Stalker glared like a doomster.

"I've got a son of ten at home who could run a Signalbox without any trouble," he sneered. "What's important is to have individuals who are accountable. I am convinced that you are not a fit and responsible person to be left in charge of running a *Shit-tip*," he scoffed. "And don't give us any of your clever claptrap either. Anybody can learn the process parrot fashion if they wanted to."

"Not if they had a speech impediment!" sparked the Flash. "What about my signatures of support?" he quaked. "There are mutants who have worked with me in excess of five years who are willing to testify that I am able to cope with the most critical emergency situations, and who have said in writing that they have every faith in my abilities."

Stalker whispered behind his upheld hand to indicate the deposition had been long overdue. They stood from the bench in unison ready to march him out of their sight.

"Concerning the correspondence with my Member of Parliament?" he interceded. "Wasn't Jones failed on his rules and ejected from the *terminus* after forty years in the grade, and reduced likewise. He resigned three weeks later and relinquished his life-pension. You informed my M.P. that I derailed a passenger train and painted a distorted picture of mayhem! How am I ever expected to escape this noxious persecution to a saner branch of humanity? Mustapha can wriggle out of anything."

223

MINISTRY OF WORK AND PENSIONS

National Council of Teachers

Pension Awards

Dear **Annoying interfering bog-roll breath,**

We have revued your pension rights for the time you have served in the teaching profession. This has been assessed as 20yrs 9mnths and 3dys. Taking into account the incremental increase, at age 65 you should be entitled to a gross annual income of £9,000 English pounds. This is partly due to breaks in your career starting with when you moved to the Irish Republic.

I hope this is satisfactory. If you have any further questions regarding your pension rights please feel free to contact us on the above number.

*If you have a bad temper please don't hesitate to intimidate your mother.

Dear Market Surgery/Managers/Doctors,

I'm just writing to inform you that for the last two years I have been my mother's main carer and means of support. We did have a visit from the Doctor the other day but I was not involved in any discussion or made aware of any issues. I am my mother's eldest son.

Just over a week ago my mum went missing in Norwich. When we wouldn't go straight to Roy's of Wroxham as she demanded mum walked off in the direction of Dereham Road saying: "you might not see me again!"

When we could not find her and she did not return home I made a 'missing person' request with the police. Fortunately, she eventually returned home safely, but was angry I had called for help. My mother is a very small frail old lady and I think she would have been very vulnerable wandering round the streets of Norwich on her own.

I would also like to make you aware that my mother's behaviour can be very difficult at times. Some of her behaviour is not really age related:

- She sometimes breaks things deliberately or hides things
- She leaves her used toilet paper in different places throughout the house
- She will not tell the truth and deliberately lies
- She sometimes comes to my door and tries to get in my room at night
- Her mood can alter very quickly and she can suddenly become very abusive

These are just a few of the behaviours I have witnessed. I have offered to drive my mum whenever she needs to go anywhere. She has written-off the garage door twice during the time I have been here and hit an island coming in our road, damaging two wheels a few months ago. My mother denies doing any of these things. She is very good at putting on an act.

Please could you involve me in the decision-making process if you can and inform me of any significant changes.

Yours Sincerely,

Andy Gallagher

Resident

(NO reply again)

*GLEN CAMPBELL

I woke up during the night singing 'Galveston.' When I switched on the TV I heard that Glen Campbell had just passed away.

IN CATHEDRAL JARS

The cards from Prue,
With pictures from her gallery,
And Pam's letters,
Rich in scenes from her family.

Roger's large and erudite hand,
Scrawled across the page,
His loving nature revealed,
For the very first time.

And Leo's inspiring words,
Giving me the will to survive,
The injustice of this prison cell,
All the way from France.

The Headmaster of my old Grammar school,
A page worn at the margins,
In the dark bunk near the ceiling,
By the window over the hospital.

My mother's screeching,
And shouting from the envelope,
How ungrateful I am,
And such a bloody disgrace.

All were saved,
Up Grapes Hill,
In the Catholic half,
At the back of the room,
On top of the Grande piano.

THE EXPERTS

1. A persistent and vicious objection to violence.
2. Laugh and clap at inappropriate moments.
3. Are difficult to diagnose but remain open to bribes.
4. Problematic personality types with a liking for mock executions.

GOLD STANDARD CHECK-LIST:
- Superficial and keen to win approval
- A low boredom threshold
- Complete lack of sincere remorse
- A parasite on the floor of the pig sty
- More versatile than the ordinary dung beetle
- Accumulates a vast amount of drivel
- Scores high in psychometric case study
- Fails to live up to low expectations
- Prefers waterboarding to skinny dipping
- Was just like others with a similar label
- Showed a very consistent pattern of behaviour
- Committed an abominable crime and sought to sweep it under the car
- Interrogated a member of the aristocracy on more than one occasion
- Was born with male characteristics and a huge pair of nuts
- Held a different opinion to the Experts
- Did not believe in the use of Corporal Punishment
- Suffered from a serious mental disorder
- Acted irrationally with no regard for the consequences
- Lacked the correct amount of grey matter
- Was wrong in the head but right in the leg
- Labelled for life and better for society
- Unable to read emotions accurately
- Did not make nice people 'happy'
- Did not resonate with other's emotions
- Would not listen to anyone wearing a badge
- No concept whatever of 'right' and 'wrong'
- Questioned everything, especially Authority
- Never made enough friends and allies
- Refused to toe-the-line since birth
- Had a dangerous addiction to drugs and net stockings
- Patronizing up to the fucking hilt
- Could not feel a degree of sympathy for his Torturers
- Compliant only with the promise of reward
- Would not accept our help or frontal lobotomy
- Incurable and possibly worse for therapy
- No cure around the corner but plenty of hogwash
- Learnt to speak normally at the cost of appearing normal

] Able to wear the mask of sanity easily
] An angel and a devil all in one body
] Kept his finger on the nuclear button at all times
] A complete loser and we know best
] Fearless dominance of the lower ranks
"If you've ever committed a crime then everything you say is wrong!"
YOU KNOW IT MAKES SENSE! Let's work together for the good of mankind.
JOIN THE PROBATION SERVICE AND WARP YOUR MIND-SET!
(Learn to kick ass where it really counts!).

227 people reached

LAST WILL

My last will and testament is that none of my family be allowed at my funeral and that my bones be scattered on the four winds. *L*

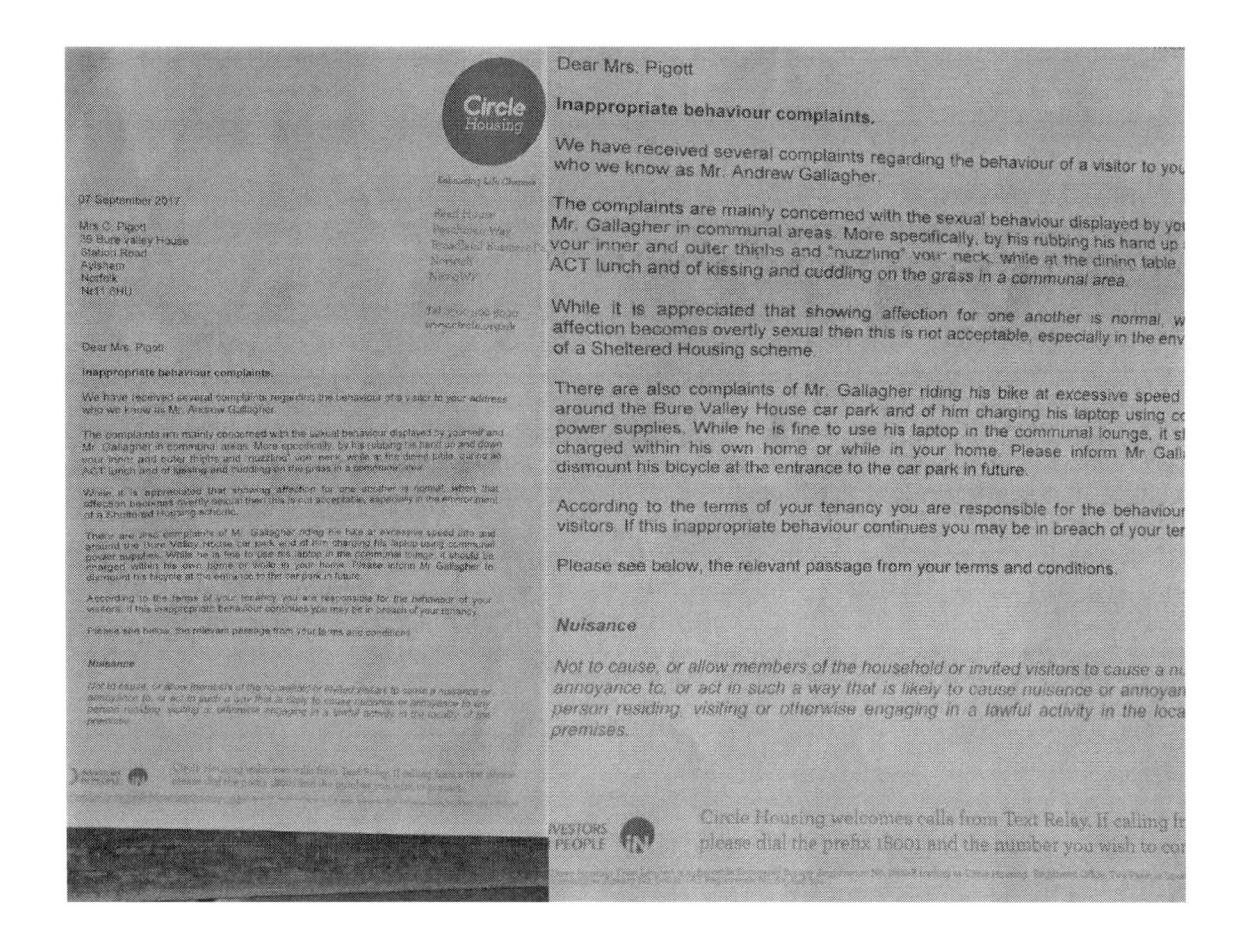

HMP Bure Valley,
Animal House.
Station Road,
Toytown.
September 2017
Re: *Snitching to the Headmaster*

Dear Siobhan,

I'm writing to *you* on behalf of myself and Christine, since Louis has 'gone away on holiday,' and we need to respond to Management as a matter of urgency about her letter. We have conducted ourselves impeccably since I started to come down again some months ago but having already been on the receiving end of malicious gossip before we did not think it would be long until certain people began their witch hunt once more. We don't have any issues with anyone and are peaceful citizens who just want to relax and get along with our friends. Neither do we hold grudges or leave the lights on in the lounge.

First of all:

1 There was no inappropriate sexual behaviour, either in the communal areas, up on the roof, or anywhere else in the vicinity. Once again, this is all about certain people with an axe-to-grind trying to give someone a bad name, but then Wherry know all about that already.

2 It is claimed that we behaved in an inappropriate *sexual* manner at an Act lunch. I'm afraid this has more to do with the 'smutty' minds of the complainants than it has to do with anything we have done wrong. No names are mentioned, but we might hazard a guess who it was. There was nothing 'overtly sexual' in anything we did. It is true that someone saw a small part of a part of my anatomy thirty years ago but surely that was over and done with a long time ago?

*Brenda Bircham at number 43 has already confirmed that she was sitting at the table when I came in to greet Christine and that there was no 'inappropriate sexual behaviour' at all. I merely put my arm around Christine in a loving embrace and kissed her head. What's wrong with these people apart from needing to get a life?

3 I have ridden my bike into the car park for years and have never injured anyone or had any type of accident. Neither have I run anyone over (A claim that I did so by Mrs Didwell, made to cause trouble in the past and which had no basis in reality). What might be viewed as 'excessive speed' to one person could be viewed as normal exercise to another. I will however dismount at the edge of the car park from now on if it makes you happy.

4 Louise has observed me quietly writing on one of the lounge tables, minding my own business, as have other Residents, but on no occasion, have I ever charged up my laptop using Wherry electricity. Another malignant and unreliable falsehood to go with all the other lies that have been told about me in the past. My laptop has always been charged up whenever I have brought it down and has its own battery pack.

5 Louise was witness to me helping Debbie (that's the former Cook who left because of malicious allegations made about her by the Didwells) in with her shopping a few days ago. She was bringing it back for her mum and seemed to be very tired. She thanked me for carrying it from the car park up to her mother's room. No mention of this? I suppose it doesn't quite fit in with all the *myth-building does it...*are you listening Mr. Yahman!

I do hope that you can refrain from 'picking' on my friend Christine because she has been extremely upset by your accusations and has already been feeling very unwell during the last few days. This sort of stress is something she could really do without. She is a decent honourable lady who has done nothing to deserve this sort of victimization and bullying, and far from being misled by me as you have insinuated in the past, has been wonderfully cared for and appreciated.

I am so sorry that you had to be involved Siobhan. One of the last Support Managers (Dorothy Hambling) became so ill she had to go off sick and leave when she got caught in the middle.

We look forward to many happy days in the future, but somehow I don't think these people are ever going to change. I presume the Managers will react in their characteristically un-biased and unprejudiced manner.

REPLY: YOUR LETTER HAS BEEN RECEIVED TODAY AND HAS BEEN PASSED ON TO OUR 'SPECIALIST' HOUSING TEAM TO FOAM AND FROTH OVER.

SECOND: Having reviewed your answers and listened to your excuses we are prepared to let Andrew continue to visit, just so long as he keeps out of the lounge area, in which case he will not be able to charge up his lap-top there and there will be no more further obscenities.

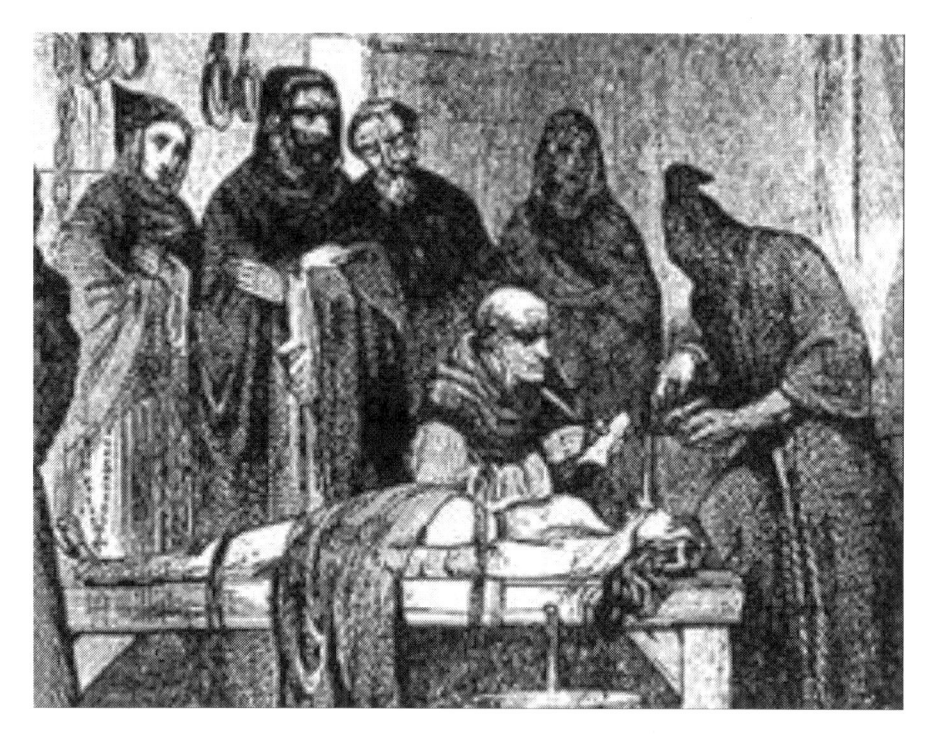

Joan of Arc's charges

Just why was little Joan of Arc burnt at the stake after being captured by the English?

- *She helped recapture Orleans*
- *She suffered from Schizophrenia?*
- *She was in link with devil*
- *She dressed herself to look like a man*
- *She didn't look good and was totally lacking in remorse*
- *She broke the faith and was very obstinate*

After days of wrangling the Judges decided that it was the wearing of men's trousers which pissed them off the most.

1. English justice at its best
2. Break the law and you will be punished
3. Still around today laying down the bull

4. Little Lord Fauntleroy

By Bird Dung | Published: September 13, 2017 | Edit

Brian used to be called 'Little Lord Fauntleroy' by his step-father, but we are not allowed to say so! I think I know what he meant though…He tells me he is thinking of going into *weed* production. It may be just a wind-up. His teeth are blackening nicely.

WHAT'S THE POINT IN DAYDREAMS

What's the point in daydreams,

If I can't see your smile,

What's the point in daydreams,

If I can't stay a while,

 And talk among the daisies,

On the winding lanes,

From our games at Belle Vue,

And back through *Miles Rough*.

What's the point in daydreams,

If I can never speak,

And tell you how it was back then,

When you stole my love.

How you took my piety,

And gave it to your friends,

And sat on that big wall nearby,

To fill my heart with tears…

How to run your neighbours down

One of the easiest ways to run your neighbour down is to hire a bike without any brakes and speed furiously all over town. If you see anyone in your path then simply shout:

"hey, get out of my way, you silly old twat."

If they wave at you, or stare cow-faced like a life-sick hedgehog in the middle of the road without moving then you can only really take one course of action. But if you do then they will have you for it! Another method might be to get Wayne Rooney to run you home when his wife is in hospital, but you would have to be wearing a short mini skirt and plenty of make-up.

*Yvonne Up-date

Your mum was right to say I suddenly disappeared at around the age of eighteen. This was about the time I became socio-phobic and could not go out of the front door without turning red. I missed out on such a lot, didn't I?

I never fell out with Walter. I was certainly having a lot of problems coping at the time. My dad had just fallen in a cement mixer and my mum was playing all sorts of tricks on me. She had a thing about pulling wires. She used to creep out of her room at night and pull all the wires out. We couldn't get a bath because she kept turning all the heating off. I also became very obsessed with my appearance, particularly the *size of my nose*, which was as great a shock to me as it was to everyone else. It grew about a quarter of an inch every day. I also had a bust up with my sister after she caught me with a pair of her knickers in my room. She told all her mates that I was a sex pervert.

At St Bedes the lads I mentioned were all members of the "Keighley lot," a gang of boys with more testosterone than Daley Thompson. I found it hard to establish my identity in the group. One day Peter Mysko gave me a real good thrashing, after I had asked him to give me my Levi jacket back several times. It had taken me ages to buy it. I'm sure I could be very irritating to some people. Peter was twice my size in the sixth form. He threw my jacket across the common room causing me to spill my coffee. I suppose it was my pride which was wounded more than my body. Until I left school I refused to speak to anyone in the group again. They tried to speak to me several times but I was so hurt by the whole experience I never forgave them. But, that was in the past Yvonne. We've all grown up a lot since then. I hope this answers your question, about me disappearing. I really did vanish I suppose, in more ways than you think...

COMPLETELY NEW MATERIAL

Reduction in numbers/cleansing of the planet
By Usuli Twelves | Published: September 28, 2017 | Edit

As we sit on the edge of a precipice waiting for the North Korean leader to decide whether to risk going for a *first strike:* possibly wiping out Washington, the ruling administration, and the President in one foul swoop, I told my beloved not to worry, and that, if the worse came to the worse we would die together with my arms wrapped tightly around her. I fear that the only solution is a military one, because the North Korean leader is not going to give back his nuclear toys willingly and if we do back down now he will know we don't have the balls we were born with. Who, besides Trump, is going to be willing to wrest these weapons from his greasy fingers? It won't be the first time in recent history that the smile has been wiped off someone's face. If China and Russia do get involved it will most likely rid the planet of billions of creatures responsible for many of the world's problems. Can I count on you to pass the buck?

JOHN SOBIESKI

The city of Vienna was besieged by Turkish forces for two months in 1683. The battle itself took place close to the city and contained about two hundred thousand Muslim warriors intent on smashing their way into the rich and fertile provinces beyond. It was a make or break time for the Habsburg dynasty and could have led to the complete collapse of Central Europe. The Viennese garrison was led by Ernst Rüdiger Graf von Starhemberg, an Austrian subject of Holy Roman Emperor Leopold I. As usual, the European armies were vastly outnumbered. Similar to the Battle of Tours in many ways, except that they had gone back to their previous strategy of attacking from the East.

Horse racing
By Bird Dung | Published: September 23, 2017 | Edit

Mum said to Chris: "You backed the wrong horse!"
I presume she is referring to myself and her ongoing snitching to the Cops.

What's the point in SHAP/another perspective?

By Surloin Steak | Published: September 25, 2017 | Edit

SHAP are supposed to represent all the Residents living at the Zoo. I spoke to one of their representatives last week and showed her a letter which we had written denying all the lies which had been told about us again. I asked her if she was coming over to talk to us at One O'clock as she'd promised. She became very cross and said that she was *right in the middle of something*.

"Ok, I can spare you both five minutes!" she fumed, and slammed the door in my face.

When she did come across she was very bossy and aggressive. She told me to remove various passages about the past in my letter. I said this was **all about the past** and refused to remove them. She became very angry when I said this. Sue said that she had never even heard of 'the Didwells...' Must be the only one who hasn't. Just before she left she strode into our bedroom and looked around. "If you're so afraid they are writing down everything you say and sending it in to Wherry, then move the fucking bed away from the wall!"

*Just a slight reminder here: that human beings are wonderful animals; benign and caring. I call them animals, but of course, they are far above the simple beasts of the plain, because they have a 'soul;' something which a kind god decided to bestow upon them after a few million years of deliberation. The worse crime any human being can commit is to force a fellow creature to have sex without consent. Killing is always wrong. You must never kill anyone. That's the most wicked thing you can ever do in my book!

Biography

Born of a virgin birth (if you believe everything your mother says) on Groundhog Day 1956, son of an English schoolteacher and regularly battered by a semi-literate Irish labourer, with a reading age of nine, and member of Sinn Fein. Was brainwashed at a local Catholic Grammar school but was expelled for setting light to the headmaster's study and refusing to get his hair cut. Suffered from socio-phobia and in 1981 entered a Signal box hermitage after doing an honours degree in Fine Art at one of the most subversive colleges in the country. Studied Astrology and the black arts but never became totally insane until meeting his former child-hood sweetheart in 1999. Was fired from his job as an Instructor in Occupational therapy after six years in the service when one of his neighbours wrote to the Trust Director to say that he was known locally as the *Phantom Groper*. Sent to prison in 2007 after sending his ex-partner a book of poetry and being caught in possession of a museum fire-arm without a licence. Returned there two years later after trying to re-contact his partner to explain that he never intended to hurt anyone.

- ✓ Retired body-builder
- ✓ Expounder of nightmares
- ✓ Slanderer of medical practitioners
- ✓ Former professional arm-wrestler
- ✓ Expert in counter intelligence (able to track down any individual across the entire planet)
- ✓ Capable of predicting close encounters and seeing over the heads of giants

Also on **AMAZON UK**:

Widening Underground Odd bent Coppers Natural Surveillance Trades of the Toadman CRIMINAL TENDENCIES OFFENSIVE BEHAVIOUR ALIEN INTELLIGENCE. Possible forthcoming titles: *The Mysterious life of Benjamin Strange/ Head of the Medusa*
BANNED FROM LIBRARIES UP AND DOWN THE COUNTRY

Reviews gratefully accepted £/$

Printed in Great Britain
by Amazon